A Blueprint for Preparing Teachers

Other titles by Marie Menna Pagliaro

Academic Success: Applying Learning Theory in the Classroom (2013)
Mastery Teaching Skills: A Resource for Implementing the Common Core State Standards (2012)
Research-Based Unit and Lesson Planning: Maximizing Student Achievement (2012)
Differentiating Instruction: Matching Strategies with Objectives (2011)
Educator or Bully?: Managing the 21st Century Classroom (2011)
Exemplary Classroom Questioning: Practices to Promote Thinking and Learning (2011)

A Blueprint for Preparing Teachers

Producing the Best Educators for Our Children

Marie Menna Pagliaro

ROWMAN & LITTLEFIELD
Lanham • Boulder • New York • London

Published by Rowman & Littlefield
A wholly owned subsidiary of The Rowman & Littlefield Publishing Group, Inc.
4501 Forbes Boulevard, Suite 200, Lanham, Maryland 20706
www.rowman.com

Unit A, Whitacre Mews, 26-34 Stannary Street, London SE11 4AB

Copyright © 2016 by Marie Menna Pagliaro

All rights reserved. No part of this book may be reproduced in any form or by any electronic or mechanical means, including information storage and retrieval systems, without written permission from the publisher, except by a reviewer who may quote passages in a review.

British Library Cataloguing in Publication Information Available

Library of Congress Cataloging-in-Publication Data

ISBN 978-1-4758-2468-1 (cloth : alk. paper) -- ISBN 978-1-4758-2469-8 (pbk. : alk. paper) -- ISBN 978-1-4758-2470-4 (electronic)

∞ ™ The paper used in this publication meets the minimum requirements of American National Standard for Information Sciences Permanence of Paper for Printed Library Materials, ANSI/NISO Z39.48-1992.

Printed in the United States of America

Everyone sits in the prison of his own ideas; he must burst it open.
—**Albert Einstein**

Contents

Introduction		ix
1	A Brief History of Teacher Education in the United States	1
2	The Teacher Education Problem	11
3	Why Teacher Education Matters	23
Part I: The Teacher Education Consortium (TEC)		**27**
4	Designing and Administering the Teacher Education Program	29
Part II: The University Program		**43**
5	The Teacher Education Candidates	45
6	The Teacher Education Curriculum	61
7	Implementing the Teacher Education Curriculum	81
8	The Teacher Educators	101
Part III: Professional Development		**109**
9	Effective Professional Development	111
References		131

Introduction

We are living in a global society in which, unfortunately, our children are not achieving as well as their counterparts in other countries. It is imperative that our children be educated to excel at a high academic level so that they will be prepared to attain a competitive advantage. To gain this advantage, we must ensure that their teachers are prepared in a way that will maximize their professional responsibilities.

Currently, teacher preparation is not succeeding to the degree necessary to provide for the needs of this global economy. Criticism of teacher education comes from many sources including non-education department university professors; school district administrators; teachers; program graduates; parents; politicians; and the business community. *A Blueprint for Preparing Teachers* presents solutions to these criticisms.

This book offers a plan designed to reflect the best research on teacher education. The components of this plan are dynamic and should change as new and solid research emerges. Though the recommendations are geared to developing pre-service undergraduate programs, other venues could also benefit.

The blueprint is directed primarily toward professors who prepare teachers and school district personnel; however, others can profit from its suggestions. Parents, community leaders, students, policy makers, and the business community will become more informed so that they, also, can become engaged in the complex processes needed to prepare teachers to be successful at the beginning and throughout their careers.

The blueprint is not for the apathetic or for those who are always ready to make excuses for the status quo. "We don't have enough time," "there isn't enough money," "we need more resources," and "this will never work" are the usual reactions.

The proposed plan is not for those who reinforce the definition of insanity by continuing to do the same thing over and over again while expecting different results.

The blueprint is not for transactional leaders. It is for transformational leaders, those who want to avoid the path to irrelevance, those who make things happen, proactive educators who are willing to create a new and bold vision and make significant changes, including, if necessary, changing themselves.

The first three chapters of *A Blueprint for Preparing Teachers* provide a framework for the rest of the text. They put into perspective the recommendations in the chapters that follow.

Chapter one places teacher education into historical context so that the reader can better understand subsequent recommendations for change.

Chapter two describes the persistent criticisms of teacher education to alert the reader to the response of the rest of the book to those criticisms.

In chapter three, empirical evidence is provided that supports the fact that the teacher is the most significant factor in student achievement and why, therefore, this teacher needs quality preparation.

After the introductory chapters, the text is presented in three parts, each reflecting one component of a set of three characteristics, all of which must be present as each contributes to the teacher education program's success. These are a meaningful collaboration among the university, school districts, and the community; an excellent ever-evolving college/university teacher education program; and a sound process for the continuing professional development of all teachers.

Each chapter within those three parts (chapters four to nine) presents background information which explains the rationale for the blueprint. Those chapters then culminate in a blueprint summary. When relevant to the text, examples called "Case in Point" are cited.

For years there have been cries for redesigning teacher preparation, yet there are still too many programs that have not responded adequately. There is no more time for delaying the change that is needed. Constructive and immediate action must be taken to better educate our teachers and keep them continuously developing. For teaching is the most important job in the world. It is the job that makes all others possible.

Marie Menna Pagliaro

Chapter One

A Brief History of Teacher Education in the United States

In Colonial America there was, surprisingly, no formal education for teachers. This lack of formality was rather remarkable considering that the colonists came from Europe, and as early as medieval Europe, the education of teachers was at the center of the university. Moreover, the license to teach was the *first* degree that the medieval universities offered. Yet, in the United States teacher education did not begin in any organized way until the last quarter of the nineteenth century.

If anything could be said about teacher education at that time, it was that it was inconsistent, diverse, and informal. Many learned, as they had for millennia before, by observing a master. The curriculum consisted of teaching students how to read, proper morals, religion, and codes of behavior.

Teacher preparation occurred in different locations. These included but were not limited to the home, church, neighbors' homes, public and private schools, private tutors, and apprenticeships. Whoever prepared the teacher corresponded to the location in which the learning took place. Obviously, in the home it was the parent, in the church it was the minister, and in the neighbor's home it was the neighbor (Labaree, 2008).

The main impetus to provide a formal system for the education of teachers came from the development of the common school system, the forerunner of our present public school system, a movement which began in the 1830s. As the common school movement spread throughout the country, this initiative brought about a corresponding demand for teachers.

To make certain that there were enough teachers and that they be prepared and certified, normal schools began to be established. The normal school was so-named because it was expected to set the norms for quality teaching. These schools were non-collegiate teacher training institutions which stressed practical education. Since at this time teaching was considered a craft, education in the normal school was rather technical, mostly involving how to do things such as open and close windows, teach the letters of the alphabet, and how to draw. This craft model was not conducive to having teachers think about *why* they were implementing various practices. In addition, normal schools were negligent in the area of having their prospective teachers master subjects taught in the elementary school.

Originally, normal schools were located in cities, within secondary schools, or within counties. But the most prestigious were the state normal schools in which the curriculum could be completed in one or two years and covered both liberal arts and pedagogical courses. In general, the normal school curriculum offered in-depth subject matter, knowledge of student development, and teaching methodology.

The main purpose of the normal school was to produce a large number of teachers to meet the demand of the growing population. Thus, it was difficult for the normal schools to meet this demand while maintaining both high-quality subject matter courses and pedagogy. The normal school was thereby faced with deciding between quality and quantity.

The social need filled by the normal schools directed the decision of their administrators to rely less on academic rigor in favor of mass production of teachers. Even though the state normal schools continued to grow, by the end of the nineteenth century they were still not able to keep up with the demand for teachers.

Concurrent with the pressure normal schools were under to mass produce teachers was the demand from their own students that these schools, which were conveniently located and relatively inexpensive compared to other types of higher education, offer more than just teacher education. Students, who desired social mobility, wanted access to other occupations. For their own survival, normal schools eventually adapted to the demands of their market, the students, who brought corresponding tuition with them.

Since the normal schools already had professors on their staff teaching courses in the liberal arts, new programs based on these liberal arts courses were relatively easy to develop. But one of the results was that the normal schools began to neglect their responsibility to provide high-quality professional teacher preparation.

Even though the normal schools offered a variety of programs other than teacher education, they were still functioning on a secondary school level. All involved—students, faculty, administrators, and communities—wanted a higher status for normal schools.

In the early part of the twentieth century, state legislatures began the transformation of normal schools into teachers colleges. These colleges were able to confer bachelor's degrees which added prestige to their programs. But as many different programs began to be offered by the teachers colleges, they developed into actual liberal arts colleges in which the preparation of teachers assumed a smaller role. This de-emphasis required a corresponding change in the institutional label. Therefore, the normal school progression went from teachers colleges to state colleges.

Beginning in the 1950s, state colleges evolved into universities which housed schools of education. University teacher education programs grew as states prescribed specific coursework for licensure. The need for teachers with college degrees was also spurred by the growth of the accreditation of secondary schools.

When, after these haphazard beginnings, teacher education finally landed in the university, there began a strained relationship between the two. It was essentially, and in most cases still is, a relationship of convenience. Teacher education provided a social need as well as a large number of students which added considerably to university coffers. This addition is not to be minimized. Revenue obtained from teacher education students was funneled into supporting other departments as well as sports programs. In turn, the university offered academic credibility and status to teacher education programs.

Even with this academic credibility, teacher education still remained on the bottom wrung of the education ladder. Teacher education enjoyed low esteem from just about everyone including politicians; practicing teachers who complained about their preparation; liberal arts professors; think tanks; graduates; students; and education professors themselves.

Labaree (2008) explains the reasons for the low status of teacher education programs.

As America grew in the [nineteenth] century, there was a great demand for teachers from both employers and school districts which were increasing the grade level of education for their students. In an attempt to provide for this need, the existing training institutions minimized standards and academic rigor for those entering the profession. Even today, teacher education is perceived as weak.

Teaching is the only "profession" that served the perceived lower levels of society, whether this be age, class, or gender. As a result of the perception of women's role in caring for the young, teaching became women's work. Women worked for half the pay that men received. Men who couldn't think of any other occupation found themselves in teaching by default.

Those who entered teaching came largely from lower middle and working classes. Since teachers dealt with the young who were not considered intellectually developed, teachers' work did not have intellectual prestige. Teacher education faculty's work, in addition to focusing on the young, was also not considered to be on a high intellectual level since it also involved the preparation of other groups that did not garner high prestige—elementary and secondary teachers and staff for preschool and day care.

Over many decades in the history of teacher education, there was a question regarding whether teaching was a profession. Throughout the years, there has developed a consensus of general attributes that define a profession. These characteristics are summed up as follows. Professions:

1. Offer an essential social service to both individuals and to the society as a whole;
2. Are concerned with a specific area of need;
3. Possess a specialized body of knowledge and skills that require continuous updating;
4. Have members who are involved in independent decision making in the service of the client;
5. Have organizations that possess autonomy to safeguard its interests as well as recommend conditions that support it such as agreed-upon standards for admission, continuance within the program, a code of ethics, licensing, and member discipline;
6. Require preparation through an extended program usually in a college, university, or professional school; and
7. Possess a high level of public confidence and trust within the profession itself and in performance of individual practitioners based upon the profession's demonstrated capacity to provide service markedly beyond that which would otherwise be available.

Which of the above criteria do you think teaching possesses? It would also be valuable to consider the British journalist Alistair Cooke's definition of a professional: "A professional is someone who can do his best work when he doesn't feel like it."

This section would not be complete unless consideration is given to the conclusion of Robert Runté (1995) on the faculty of the University of Lethbridge in England regarding whether teaching is a profession.

He states:

> Is teaching a profession? ... This is a trick question, and ... teachers must not allow themselves to get tricked again. *There is no such thing as a profession.* The only feature that ever really distinguished the professions from other occupations was the "professional" label itself. What we are is knowledge workers, and as such we have a responsibility to both ourselves and to the public to become reflective practitioners. As reflective practitioners, we can reassert, first our ability, and then our right, to assume responsibility for the educational enterprise. (p. 34, italics in original)

Whether one believes that teaching is or is not a profession, there is agreement that teaching requires a code of ethics. The National Education

Association developed a code of ethics for teachers (www.nea.org/home/ 30442.htm). The American Association of Educators also developed a code of ethics (www.aaeteachers.org/index.php/about-us/aae-code-of-ethics). Compare the two codes on these websites to note similarities and differences. Individual states have also developed codes of ethics for teachers. It would be valuable to read the code of ethics of the state where you reside, teach, or plan to teach.

ALTERNATE ROUTES TO TEACHER CERTIFICATION

For many years it was possible to get a teaching certificate without going through the traditional route, completing a state-registered teacher education program. Certification could be achieved by taking a specified number of education courses or credits which varied by states. Later, master of arts in teaching programs developed at universities allowed students who had achieved bachelor degrees without any education courses to complete these courses and, therefore, achieve certification on the graduate level. Thus, master of arts in teaching programs offered master degrees and certification at the same time.

About forty years ago, the need for teachers in rural and urban areas and in critical subject areas such as mathematics and science led to the emergence of less traditional models for achieving certification. The model that has acquired the most attention is Teach for America (TFA), which has had a large impact on the national discussion regarding how to prepare teachers.

Though much of the publicity given to TFA comes from the fact that it has drawn large numbers of graduates from elite colleges and universities into its program, of greater impact has been TFA's attention given to the *results* of their graduates' instruction—student achievement. This focus has forced traditional teacher education programs to look at this same question to determine how well their graduates succeed in promoting the achievement of their own students, thus providing more accountability for traditional teacher education program results.

ACCREDITATION OF TEACHER EDUCATION PROGRAMS

As in other higher education fields that prepare professionals, teacher education has used accreditation as a means of controlling the quality of its program and its graduates. (It is important to note that not all states require accreditation for teacher education programs.) In 1948, the American Association of Colleges for Teacher Education (AACTE) began accrediting institutions that prepared teachers. By 1950, it had issued the first of several versions of Revised Standards and Policies for Accrediting Colleges for Teacher

Education. In 1954, perhaps recognizing the conflict of interest inherent in being the organization of those institutions preparing teachers and also being responsible for managing the accrediting process, AACTE gave up responsibility for accreditation.

As a result, the National Council for the Accreditation of Teacher Education (NCATE) was created and has dominated the accrediting process at the national level. Over the years, several versions of its standards, policies, and practices have emerged. Many teacher education programs worked collaboratively with NCATE.

In the early 1990s, an alternative accrediting body, the Teacher Education Accreditation Council (TEAC), was initiated and eventually enlisted close to one hundred institutions. It became evident that having these two competing accrediting agencies was counterproductive, and eventually NCATE and TEAC merged into the Council for the Accreditation of Educator Preparation (CAEP), which is currently the sole agency for those who seek accreditation for their programs.

As NCATE and TEAC before it, CAEP requires that teacher education institutions desiring accreditation complete a self-study and host a site visit, at which time the visitors decide based on evidence of teacher candidate performance and program data for self-improvement and commitment to quality whether CAEP standards for accreditation have been met.

CAEP aims to raise teacher education candidates' performance as practitioners in the nation's pre-kindergarten to grade twelve (P-12) schools and to implement high standards supporting the evidence the field relies on to verify its claims of quality. By meeting these goals, NCATE and TEAC leaders believe that the stature of the profession will be raised.

The five standards CAEP currently purports to hold programs (or units) accountable for can be found at their new website, www.caepnet.org. These include the following.

Standard 1: Content and Pedagogical Knowledge

The provider (teacher education program) ensures that candidates develop a deep understanding of the critical concepts and principles of their discipline and, by completion are able to use discipline-specific practices flexibly to advance the learning of all students toward attainment of college-and-career-readiness standards.

Standard 2: Clinical Partnerships and Practice

The provider ensures that effective partnerships and high-quality clinical practice are central to preparation so that candidates develop the knowledge, skills, and professional dispositions necessary to demonstrate positive impact on all P-12 students' learning and development.

Standard 3: Candidate Quality, Recruitment, and Selectivity

The provider demonstrates that the quality of candidates is a continuing and purposeful part of its responsibility from recruitment at admission, through the progression of courses and clinical experiences, and to decisions that completers are prepared to teach effectively and are recommended for certification. The provider demonstrates that development of candidate quality is the goal of educator preparation in all phases of the program. This process is ultimately determined by a program's meeting of Standard 4.

Standard 4: Program Impact

The provider demonstrates the impact of its completers on P-12 student learning and development, classroom instruction, and schools, and the satisfaction of its completers with the relevance and effectiveness of their preparation.

Standard 5: Provider Quality Assurance and Continuous Improvement

The provider maintains a quality assurance system comprised of valid data from multiple measures, including evidence of candidates' and completers' positive impact on P-12 student learning and development. The provider supports continuous improvement that is sustained and evidence-based, and that evaluates the effectiveness of its completers. The provider uses the results of inquiry and data collection to establish priorities, enhance program elements and capacity, and test innovations to improve completers' impact on P-12 student learning and development.

CAEP will offer three accreditation options: Continuous Improvement, Inquiry Brief, and Transformation Initiative. Regardless of the option a preparation program chooses to follow, it will provide evidence (1) that it meets the CAEP standards, (2) that there is a functioning quality control system used to collect and analyze valid and reliable evidence of candidate learning, and (3) that program planning and decisions are based on evidence of candidate learning.

CAEP, however, is not without growing pains. The AACTE articulated its concern regarding CAEP's recommendations for candidate selection, program outcome measurements, and recognition of top performing programs (Sawchuk, 2013). Two years later, the AACTE expressed a "crisis of confidence" in the accreditor, citing costs, standards, and the accreditation process itself, among other concerns (Sawchuk, 2015a). And both teachers and teacher educators complained that CAEP's standards stifled innovation, creativity, and even promoted an ideological agenda.

Rather stunningly, in May 2015 CAEP removed its president, replacing him with an interim president (Sawchuk, 2015c). Subsequently, CAEP's Board of Directors reaffirmed its commitment to selectivity criteria and explored ways to implement effective practices as it continued to elicit feedback on its proposals. Five months later the interim president was appointed the official president, a signal that CAEP is on its way to settling its accreditation requirements.

The federal government, in an attempt to ensure that teachers are classroom-ready, is also providing its own standards for the teaching profession (U.S. Department of Education, 2014). The federal proposal would require that states report annually on teacher preparation program performance based on the following:

- Employment outcomes: New teacher placement and three-year retention rates in high-need schools and in all schools;
- New teacher and employer feedback: Surveys on the effectiveness of preparation;
- Student learning outcomes: Impact of new teachers as measured by student growth, teacher evaluation, or both; and
- Assurance of specialized accreditation or evidence that a program produces high-quality candidates.

A proposed regulation fact sheet on federal proposals can be downloaded at www.ed.gov/teacherprep. Their teacher education standards are currently in a state of flux with some complaining that the federal proposals are too strict while CAEP standards are not strict enough (Schaffhauser, 2015). There are also complaints about federal overreach, unintended consequences, and whether or not the federal government should be involved at all (Goodwin, 2015; Robinson, 2015). Some groups have expressed concerns over the cost of the federal proposals as well as their validation (Stratford, 2015). As of this writing, time is still being allowed for further suggestions and recommendations before the federal (and CAEP) proposals are finalized.

In December of 2015 President Obama signed into law the Every Student Succeeds Act (ESSA), a rewrite of the fifty-year-old Elementary and Secondary Education Act (ESEA). The Every Student Succeeds Act replaces No Child Left Behind (NCLB) while retaining its key elements, in particular, yearly testing. The new law gives states and school districts a larger say in educational policy.

Relevant to this book, however, are the implications of the ESSA to teacher preparation. The law allows "academies" to offer teacher education programs. Moreover, these "academies", which are alternative programs, could exist within or outside of higher education. The traditional teacher education community has expressed its concerns regarding the funding of these programs along with quality and regulatory issues. Stay tuned.

EDTPA (TEACHER PERFORMANCE ASSESSMENT)

Recognizing the challenge that novice teachers have in meeting the academic needs of all students, and pressuring teacher education programs to be more accountable in meeting this challenge, Stanford University and the AACTE, with substantial input from teachers and teacher educators, partnered to give teacher education programs access to a multiple measure assessment system aligned to state and national standards in order to guide curriculum development and practice. This partnership resulted in edTPA, which aims to ensure that novice teachers can teach every student effectively and improve student achievement.

To this end, candidates have to show that they have both the knowledge and skills to be effective. They have to demonstrate high cognitive skills including analysis and synthesis. Using their videos, candidates have to prove that they can create lessons that engage a wide variety of learners, promote their understanding, and determine lesson effectiveness by identifying strengths and areas that need improvement.

edTPA is new in that it is the *first standards-based assessment* currently available in the United States and is designed to be used as a portfolio-based assessment for pre-service teacher candidates. To many, it is the equivalent of a bar exam for entrance into the profession.

As in deciding whether to seek accreditation for their teacher education institutions, states can also decide whether to pursue edTPA. At this time, fewer than ten states have opted to require that their universities meet edTPA assessments.

According to the website, http://edtpa.aacte.org/about-tpa,

> edTPA is transformative for prospective teachers because the process requires candidates to actually demonstrate the knowledge and skills required to help all students learn in real classrooms. edTPA is intended to be used as a summative assessment given at the end of a educator preparation program for teacher licensure or certification and to support state and national program accreditation. edTPA complements existing entry-level assessments that focus on basic skills or subject-matter knowledge. It is comparable to the licensing exams that demand applications of skills in other professions, such medical licensing exams, the architecture exam, or the bar exam in law. It is designed to evaluate how teacher candidates plan and teach lessons in ways that make the content clear and help diverse students learn, assess the effectiveness of their teaching, and adjust teaching as necessary.

edTPA is a subject-specific assessment with versions in [twenty-seven] different teaching fields covering Early Childhood, Elementary, Middle Childhood and Secondary. edTPA includes a review of a teacher candidate's authentic teaching materials as the culmination of a teaching and learning process that documents and demonstrates each candidate's ability to effectively teach subject matter to all students. edTPA doesn't ask candidates to do anything that most aren't already doing in their preparation programs, but it does ask for greater support for and demonstration of these skills that research and educators find are essential to student learning.

edTPA is not about theory. It goes beyond classroom credits to ask teacher candidates to demonstrate what they can and will do on the job, translating into practice what research shows improves learning.

Currently, teacher education institutions are reviewing their programs and deciding whether to seek only the program approval required by their state or whether to submit their programs for certification (CAEP) and/or prepare their students for the rigorous assessments required by edTPA.

Chapter Two

The Teacher Education Problem

Hardly a month goes by without a major book, article, or report regarding the preparation of teachers. The words reform, restructure, reorganize, revamp, transform, overhaul, and their equivalents appear ubiquitously as part of the titles or subtitles. Moreover, this is not a recent phenomenon; these publications have been appearing for years.

In addition to books on how to prepare teachers, there has been no dearth of books and reports critical of the teacher education enterprise itself. Merely reading the titles tells the story. Some of the titles include *Education Rot* (Williams, 2013), *Ed School Follies: The Miseducation of America's Teachers* (Kramer, 2008), *Teacher Education: Coming up Empty* (Walsh, 2006), *Ed Schools: The Real Shame of the Nation* (Stotsky, 2006), and *Master of None* (Fitzhugh, 2006). And the list goes on.

When examining the content of these books, the gist of their criticism is essentially the same: Education schools have abandoned the teaching of information (knowledge) in favor of developing self-esteem, promoting indiscriminate passing of courses, diversity, and the reforming of society.

Conservative columnist George Will (2013) in an article, "Propaganda as Pedagogy," complains, "The real vocation of some people entrusted with delivering primary and secondary education is to validate this proposal: The three R's—formerly reading, 'riting, and 'rithmetic—now are racism, reproduction and recycling." He goes on to criticize diversity:

> Higher education, from which much . . . diversity and sensitivity nonsense trickles down, cries poverty while spending lavishly on administrative overhead irrelevant to its teaching and research missions. [While] the University of California at San Diego was pruning academic offerings [in 2011], it created a "vice chancellor for equity, diversity, and inclusion" to augment a diversity apparatus that included an assistant vice chancellor for diversity; faculty advis-

ers, staff, graduate and undergraduate diversity coordinators and liaisons; (and) a director of development for diversity initiatives. (p. A11)

Will (2013) offers the following on propaganda:

> No corner of the country is immune to propaganda pretending to be pedagogy. Twenty-five years ago, President Reagan, paraphrasing Education Secretary William Bennett, said: "If you serve a child a rotten hamburger in America, federal, state and local agencies will investigate you, summon you, close you down, whatever. But if you provide a child with a rotten education, nothing happens, except that you are liable to be given more money to do it with. (p. A11)

Critics continue to protest that most professors have abandoned scholarship in favor of promoting propaganda and that which is politically correct, and that education school faculty offer a gap between what they believe and the concerns expressed by parents, teachers, and students themselves. Schools of education grant final degrees devoid of substantive value.

Education professors have been described as "educrats," those who are so process-oriented that they focus on how students learn as opposed to *what* they learn. Educrats are group thinkers who promote "pernicious" ideology—multicultural sensitivity, community building, collaborative grouping, and brainstorming without developing content about which to brainstorm. There is a de-emphasis on knowledge in favor of student-centered learning and producing teachers as facilitators who assist students in discovering knowledge for themselves. Teachers are trained as change agents whose mission is to work toward social justice and equity in the classroom.

There is a focus on theory without a corresponding weight on how to implement that theory. Schools (divisions/departments) of education provide low academic preparation of teachers who enter the program with low SAT scores and leave with low GRE scores. In short, the curriculum of education schools, and universities in general, is infamous for its lack of rigor, domination by political correctness, and emphasis on theory.

CASE IN POINT 1

Comedian Jerry Seinfeld appeared on ESPNU and ESPN Radio's "The Herd with Colin Cowherd" on June 4, 2015, and spoke on how other comedians have told him to not do comedy at college campuses because they are so politically correct now. According to Seinfeld, people do not even know what they are talking about when they throw out terms such as "racist" or "sexist," and this has made its way into colleges, making them too politically correct to do comedy.

Comedian Chris Rock, in a 2015, wide-ranging Vulture interview, was asked for his thoughts on the controversy a year earlier about talk show host and comedian

Bill Maher speaking at UC Berkeley's commencement. Ironically, considering that this is the fiftieth anniversary year of the Free Speech Movement at Berkeley, students disinvited Maher over remarks he had made about Islam that some found "racist and bigoted."

Curiously, it was the university that stepped up in support of free speech over student objections; the administration reinstated Maher's invitation, asserting that it fully respects and supports Maher's right to express his opinions and does not intend to "shy away from hosting speakers who some deem provocative."

"Well, I love Bill," Rock answered, "but I stopped playing colleges, and the reason is because they're way too conservative." Politically conservative, not in their political views—not like they're voting Republican—but in their social views and their willingness not to offend anybody. Kids raised on a culture of "We're not going to keep score in the game because we don't want anybody to lose." Or just ignoring race to a fault. You can't say "the black kid over there." No, it's "the guy with the red shoes." You can't even be offensive on your way to being inoffensive.

Maher wasn't the only commencement speaker to have been confronted by politically correct sensibilities: Condoleezza Rice at Rutgers University, International Monetary Fund head Christine Lagarde at Smith College, and former UC Berkeley Chancellor Robert Birgeneau at Haverford College were all successfully shut down. Ayaan Hirsi Ali, women's rights proponent and fierce critic of Islam, was denied an honorary degree at Brandeis for similar reasons.

Political correctness, Chris Rock said, is "stronger than ever." The atmosphere on today's campuses is that of intolerance of anyone and anything that could conceivably give offense, that challenges students' biases and makes them feel uncomfortable. Thanks to the comforting embrace of Orwellian speech codes, safe spaces, and trigger warnings, too many young people place a high priority on the protection of their feelings and beliefs. They're wary of testing received wisdom and expanding their horizons, and they cling to favored illusions while wrapping themselves in the force-field of victim status.

The result is a reflexive sensitivity that renders the comedy routine of someone like Rock completely toothless and pointless; hence, no more college tours.

Rock told his Vulture interviewer that he began to notice this dismal state of affairs "about eight years ago. Probably a couple of tours ago. It was just like, This is not as much fun as it used to be. I remember talking to George Carlin before he died [in 2008] and him saying the exact same thing."

Carlin, of course, was an uncompromising champion for free speech. "Political correctness is America's newest form of intolerance," Carlin once complained, "and it's especially pernicious because it comes disguised as tolerance." He was surprised by the censorship from "the politically correct people on the campuses," and groused about the tortured, evasive wording forced upon everyone by the "Political Language Police" in a misguided attempt to avoid being judgmental. "Politically correct language cripples discourse, creates ugly language, and is generally stupid," he declared.

Universities exist—in theory, anyway—to open up students' minds, not circumscribe them. But political correctness is so much the "new normal" that the students themselves have become their own intellectual jailers. It may take another couple of generations of hard work to dismantle that and reopen the American mind. Too bad Chris Rock abandoned that field, because comedy is a uniquely powerful tool for challenging one's perspective and saying what cannot be said (Schramm, 2015).

CASE IN POINT 2

A woman who had achieved full professor status at a college that prepared teachers retired. She was subsequently enlisted to supervise student teachers at a major university that prepares teachers. Since the woman's husband had been a successful principal at a charter school, she listed him as a speaker on the topic of charter schools for one of the student teaching seminar sessions. When the administration of the university saw the name and listing, they advised the woman that they did not discuss nor approve of charter schools at their university and demanded that she take her husband off the list of speakers.

Educational researcher Diane Ravitch (2003) provided evidence that pedagogical leaders have given credibility to dubious research findings *grounded more in ideology than in data*. In addition, she stated that unlike those in medicine who keep up with the latest medical research, educators do not exhibit the need to know the latest educational research.

Research reported by Sawchuk (2010) indicated that education professors do believe in progressive education principles with 68 percent seeing their role to prepare teachers to be change agents. A total of 44 percent believed in teaching phonics in the early years, 42 percent thought it was important to train teachers how to plan lessons and manage time, and 36 percent believed that children should memorize mathematics facts such as the multiplication tables.

Leo (2005) accused the cultural left of using disposition theory to enforce political conformity in education schools, which he regards as liberal monocultures. He charged one of the accrediting bodies at that time, the National Council for Accreditation of Teacher Education (see chapter 1), of wanting future teachers to be judged by their "knowledge, skills, and dispositions." These dispositions demanded support for diversity and a culturally left agenda. Future teachers had to oppose "institutional racism, classism, and heterosexism," which led them to believe that their not agreeing with or questioning these would make classroom dissent dangerous for them.

CASE IN POINT 3

A teacher in one of the colleges as part of the City University of New York showed *Fahrenheit 9/11*, Michael Moore's movie. The teacher dismissed "white English" as the "language of the oppressors." Five students filed written complaints about this comment. After receiving no formal reply from the college, one student was told to leave the college and take a similar course at a community college. Two of the students were accused of plagiarism and their grade reduced by one letter. When the students requested to present a witness, tape recorder, or lawyer to meet with the dean regarding the matter, they were refused.

A history professor at the college who defended the complaining students became a target himself. He was warned that he might be investigated by a Faculty Integrity Committee after an article he wrote attacking dispositions theory as a form of mind control appeared in *Inside Higher Ed*. In the professor's defense, the Foundation for Individual Rights in Education stated: "_____ College must confirm that it tolerates dissent, that it is not conducting another secret investigation of one of its own professors." The college has "disavowed any secret investigation."

CASE IN POINT 4

A college of education on the West Coast threatened to terminate the matriculation of a student for failing four "professional disposition evaluations." The student had expressed his opposition to affirmative action and to the adoption of children by gays. Even though this student had good grades and was considered highly intelligent even by his critics, he was given a failing Professional Disposition Evaluation after the professor noticed the statement "diversity is perversity" written in his textbook.

The student was threatened with expulsion if he did not sign a contract agreeing to mandatory diversity training, the completion of various projects at the discretion of the faculty, and above-average scrutiny during student teaching. When the Foundation for Individual Rights in Education entered the dispute, the faculty told the student he did not have to sign the contract and would not lose matriculation. However, the faculty and the dean did not agree to avoid using dispositions theory for apparently ideological purposes.

CASE IN POINT 5

A retired gentleman who possessed a doctorate in music decided to keep his brain active by registering for an online course in American music at a major university in the Northeast. During the first session, the professor tried to make the point that

Native American music was *superior* to Western music. The gentleman and more than half of the students immediately withdrew from the course.

CASE IN POINT 6

Josh Hedtke, in a report posted by Aleister on June 11, 2015, indicated that at faculty leader training sessions initiated by University of California President Janet Napolitano, and conducted during the 2014-2015 academic year in nine of the ten University of California campuses, faculty were to avoid "microaggression" statements. Microaggressions were examples of subconscious racism.

Some of the statements/questions that California professors were not to say were:

> "America is the land of opportunity."
> "Anyone can succeed in this society, if they work hard enough."
> "Where are you from or where were you born?"
> "Affirmative action is racist."
> "When I look at you, I don't see color."

These statements were particular targets because they promote the "myth of meritocracy" or represent "statements which assert that race or gender does not play a role in life successes."

To continue with the teacher education criticism, the American Educational Research Association (2005) itself confirmed that there is scant empirical evidence to support the methods used to prepare the nation's teachers. And education schools are unwilling to evaluate empirically the effects of theories and practices that they promote before dismissing disliked theories and practices that are supported by large bodies of empirical evidence.

Of all the criticized practices education professors promote that offer less evidence of pedagogical effectiveness, three of them stand out.

The first is that these professors are bent on ignoring solid gains by students when the direct teaching method is employed and foster instead constructivist curriculum implementation. In a summary of research on direct instruction, Ellis (2001) states:

> It is difficult to know how to conclude a chapter devoted to a topic that has such a solid record of supportive evidence behind it but which is not particularly liked by large numbers of teachers. Such is the case with Direct Instruction. Well, broccoli has a pretty solid record, and yet it is easy to find people who don't like and won't eat the green stuff. . . . Maybe Direct Instruction is the broccoli of educational practice, good for you but not everybody's favorite dish (pp. 226–27).

The second practice that education professors promote is the whole language approach to teaching reading as opposed to the teaching of phonics. Yet, in a synthesis of research by the renowned reading specialist Chall (2000), published posthumously, it was reported that traditional approaches to reading (direct instruction, phonics, and decoding) were more effective as compared to more progressive approaches (whole-language, emphasis on meaning, and phonics as needed).

Particularly disturbing is the third practice for which there is an abundance of evidence pointing to methodology that produces the best results for poor children being actually denounced by social justice advocates as racist and oppressive. On the contrary, there is no evidence that social justice pedagogy raises academic achievement of minority and poor students (Stern, 2006). Yet this pedagogy persists to the point that legislators have been encouraged to request that their state education boards compose new guidelines discouraging teaching for social justice and forbidding teachers to indoctrinate students with their own politics, regardless of whether it is right or left.

According to critics, the results of these favored practices of education professors have fostered within the general population the growth of tutorial programs, charter schools, and home schooling.

In summary, Kozloff (2002) offers a ten-point critique of education schools (departments, divisions).

1. Education schools offer little convincing evidence that new graduates know how to teach.
2. New graduates are not taught exactly how to teach and are ill-prepared when they have their own classrooms.
3. The dominant majority of professors in typical education schools (i.e., progressive and constructivist) arrogate to themselves and to their schools a mission and social agenda contrary to what is wanted by the public.
4. Education school teacher training curricula rest on and are misguided by empirically weak and logically flawed faddish constructivist speculations.
5. When teachers use so-called developmentally appropriate, progressive curricula and teaching methods taught in education schools (such as whole language approach to beginning reading, constructivist math, and inquiry approaches to literature and science), a substantial proportion of school children do not learn.
6. Education schools do not adequately teach students the logic of scientific reasoning.
7. Education professors typically read little that challenges what they already believe.

8. Education professors regard their activities as a form of play.
9. Education schools attempt to maintain the appearance of being self-reflective, in touch with scientific research in the field, and responsive to the needs of schools by conjuring up one after another innovation or initiative.
10. Unlike medicine, structural engineering, and food science, education schools do not have a knowledge base shared within and across schools, and that rests on scientific research.

There is no doubt that many of these criticisms of teacher education programs are valid. But what most critics and the public in general do not understand is that teaching is a most complex act and a difficult skill to master. There are an infinite number of variables interacting at any one moment. Effective teaching demands intensive training, practice, and continuous professional development.

Consider the point made by Labaree (2008):

> Teaching is an extraordinarily difficult job that looks easy, which is a devastating combination for its professional standing and for the standing of its professional educators. Why is teaching so difficult? One reason is that teaching cannot succeed without the compliance of the student. Most professions can carry out their work independent of the client: surgeons operate on the anesthetized and lawyers defend the mute. But teachers can only accomplish their goals if students are willing to learn. They exert their efforts to motivate student compliance in the task of learning, but they cannot on their own make learning happen. (pp. 298–99)

Labaree (2008) goes on to say that unlike clients of lawyers and physicians, pre-college students are generally not in classrooms under their own volition and do not seek out learning on their own. Also, clients of lawyers and patients of physicians are dealt with one at a time, whereas elementary teachers interact with about twenty-five students at one time. And secondary teachers work with approximately 125 students per day.

Teaching is perceived as easy because everyone has gone to school and, therefore, considers him/herself an expert on the subject. Those who pursue teacher education programs, since they have observed teachers over a long period of time, often enter thinking they already know how to teach. This exposure does not exist in other professions.

In addition, to many, teaching seems to be inborn and not necessarily a skill to be learned. These perceptions give little authority or prestige to teacher education programs. And whereas clients of other professions return as necessary, teachers succeed by making the return of their students unnecessary. In short, "Teaching is . . . a very difficult form of professional practice, which makes teacher preparation equally difficult" (Labaree, 2008, p. 299).

Critics of the education school critics counter with arguments of their own.

1. There are major differences between teaching college/university students and those in the elementary/secondary schools, the latter the focus of education schools. University professors have students who opt to be in college and are more motivated in pursuing an education. These students are more selective. And the fact that they are older makes them developmentally different from children and early adolescents. Place these non-education professors with a group of eighth graders in a public school and see how well these professors fare without specialized training. And even more difficult, place non-education professors in charge of a kindergarten classroom and see what comes of it.

2. While non-education professors have continually criticized education programs, it may come as a surprise to them that they also are also in the field of education and that they teach. Tierney (2013) discusses a Gallup poll showing that student engagement goes from 76 percent in elementary school to 44 percent in high school. He blames this drop on outdated teaching paradigms *which continue into the universities*. Therefore, professors should be examining more closely what they are doing in their college classrooms to communicate more effectively with their students and keep them engaged. And it has been demonstrated many times that the most effective teaching is based on positive relationships in the classroom (Gardner, 2014a). Negative relationships will negate the benefits of instructional strategies shown to be most effective (Marzano, 2007).

How often have students stated that some of their professors knew their subject but just couldn't get it across? For years an emphasis in the university on subject matter knowledge has trumped pedagogy. But the truth is that methods matter and what college professors do in their classes does make a difference in how their students learn.

Example: Since the lecture is still the predominant means of instruction in the college classroom, consider how the method of delivering a lecture can be improved by using several validated procedures.

Assuming that the content was thoroughly prepared, the person delivering the lecture:

- introduced the lecture with a hook that engaged the students;
- organized the content in approximately ten-minute segments;
- organized the appropriate amount of material that could be processed;
- requested that the students summarize major points at the end of each segment;
- incorporated visuals;

- offered vivid examples;
- provided advance organizers;
- asked questions intermittently;
- varied the presentation; and
- presented content with enthusiasm.

How many times has anyone attended a college lecture that offered this type of delivery? What would have been the result with respect to learning the content by attending a lecture that had the above attributes? And how would the content presented in any lecture be better internalized through a prepared video which students can watch when and as often as they want at their convenience when offered as part of blended learning?

Sanchez (2015) reported on the best college professors. Besides knowing their disciplines, effective professors consider the intended outcomes of their instruction; think about how to assist students to achieve; consider how to give students feedback; allow their students to try, fail, and try again; trust students and treat them with respect; allow students to collaborate to wrestle with problems; and lead students to take control of their own education. These are just some of what pre-kindergarten to grade twelve candidates are taught to do.

3. Regarding the critique that education schools do not have a knowledge base they teach their students derived from empirical evidence, examine the work of Marzano, Pickering, and Pollack (2001) and Marzano (2007), who have made amazing strides in this area. (However, Marzano [2009] has asserted that teachers most often implement instruction in a classroom by themselves and do so without definite methodology that works all the time. Marzano is still struggling with questions regarding which instructional strategies are more effective in different subject areas, grade levels, and with students from different backgrounds and different aptitudes.)

And brain research has provided the hard science that has verified the soft science teacher effectiveness research of the 1970s (Jensen, 1998, 2005).

4. Also, there is no one who will doubt how education schools have advanced the teaching of students with exceptionalities. If it weren't for the different methods used with these students, they would be falling through the cracks within our educational system as they had been forty years ago when even some of the brightest would have been labeled "slow" or "retarded." Regarding their criticism of group work, non-education professors show their ignorance regarding how non–English-speaking students and other students with difficulties can participate in learning activities more freely in groups and with more confidence, thus improving their academic achievement.

5. While liberals in the past had always prided themselves in fostering the growth of universities, believing in the value of transmitting the culture, individual liberty, reason and argument, civility, representation in institu-

tions, and the rule of law, for the past fifty years, liberal professors have instead been promoting a social agenda and political correctness which has permeated academia and the culture. Eighty-five percent of professors identify themselves as liberals. They have not welcomed open debate on many topics, most frequently presenting a monolithic point of view and ridiculing those who hold opposing views. Students have been indoctrinated by not being exposed to different ideas, by not being taught how to question, by not role playing by defending views opposite theirs, and by not being taught how to come up with facts that test different opinions. In short, students have been taught *what* to think, not *how* to think. So how can these students develop critical thinking, universally recognized as an important twenty-first century skill, in their students?

The culture of a university is reflected in its commencement speakers. In a recent survey conducted by the Young America's Foundation, it was reported that liberal commencement speakers in the top one hundred universities outnumbered conservatives six to one (Morris, 2015). Furthermore, liberal speakers outnumbered conservatives nine to one in the top fifty universities, with no conservative and nine liberal speakers among the top ten universities (one with no speaker).

The origin of the word "university" implies a universe of research and thought. Many universities boast this diversity of thought in their missions but are short on delivery. Textbook publishers have been quick to pick up on what professors want. And suddenly these professors are "shocked, shocked, shocked" that the teachers who have emerged from their colleges and universities and many of the public schools themselves have adopted the same non-questioning ideology and have produced students who cannot think critically.

6. Have non-education professors heard of learning standards, especially the Common Core State Standards? Anyone who actually examines these standards will see that they have a solid knowledge base that teachers must teach.

7. All professors must ask themselves who fostered the self-concept movement, one that encouraged students to feel good about themselves, regardless of what they achieved. Who endorsed the dropping of grades? Who de-emphasized the education of the gifted in the name of equality? And who defended the lack of stigmas attached to poor behavior? Those guilty should not now be criticizing the results of the very policies and vision they sponsored.

8. Non-education professors should become aware of the fact that candidates in teacher education programs recognize that positive relationships with students promote cognition, learn how to engage students in the learning process, exhibit sensitivity to cultural differences, and cater to the different ways students learn. These are all areas in which all college faculty should be aware and involved with their own students.

The arguments persist. Many of the problems identified in this chapter should be resolved or at least assuaged with the blueprint recommendations offered in this book.

Chapter Three

Why Teacher Education Matters

Over the past three decades, much research has been dedicated to determining what factors affect student achievement. One of the most significant studies conducted regarding what contributes most to student learning was led by William Sanders, a statistician at the University of Tennessee, and reported by Sanders and Rivers (1996).

Beginning in 1992, the State of Tennessee commissioned Dr. Sanders to analyze the teaching performance of its thirty thousand teachers and the records of its six million students. In an interview conducted with Marks (2000), Dr. Sanders explained how he and his team examined class size, school location (rural, urban, suburban), ethnicity, students heterogeneously and homogeneously grouped, amount of expenditure per pupil, and percentage of students eligible for free lunch. Much to his surprise, he discovered that *teacher effectiveness* is ten to twenty times as significant as any of these other effects. He was able to quantify just how much teachers matter and demonstrate that a "bad" teacher can deter the progress of a child for at least four years.

Wright, Horn, and Sanders (1997), in a subsequent study involving sixty thousand students, came to the same conclusions. As a result, they recommended that the best way to improve education is to improve teacher effectiveness.

Sanders and his colleagues were not the only researchers to emphasize the importance of teachers' performance on student achievement. Haycock (1998), working in Boston and Dallas, reported similar findings, with effective teachers having a profound influence.

The National Commission on Teaching and America's Future (1996) issued its influential report which indicated that *what teachers know and can do is the most important influence on student learning*. Pipho (1998) concluded that the effectiveness of the individual classroom teacher was the single largest factor affecting student growth, with prior achievement, heterogeneity, and class size paling in comparison with teacher performance.

Nye, Konstantopoulos, and Hedges (2004) verified that what teachers do in the classroom has a direct effect on student achievement. Schneider (2015) reported research confirming that among in-school variables, it is the quality of the teacher that exerts the strongest influence on student success.

After studying in-service training and district innovations, Joyce and Showers (2002) determined that the key to the growth of students is the growth of teachers. Despite increasing school safety, requiring uniforms, changing the curriculum, offering afterschool programs, reducing class size, and increasing a lot more spending per pupil, Felch, Song, and Poindexter (2010) indicated that *the only progress that came in a chronically underperforming middle school was bringing in effective teachers.*

Hanushek (2011), in his own analysis, concluded that an effective teacher, which he defines as one in the top 15 percent for performance based on student achievement, can in one year take an average student from the fiftieth to the fifty-eighth percentile or above. The implication is that the same student with a teacher in the bottom 15 percent will end up below the forty-second percentile. And when assigned a teacher in the bottom 5 percent, a student in the middle of the distribution could fall to the bottom third by the end of the school year.

Hanushek's research also took into account student backgrounds and initial knowledge, and applies to urban, suburban, and rural schools. He even goes on to calculate the economic impact of effective and ineffective teaching. Hanushek's study concluded that teachers in the top 15 percent (for performance based on student achievement) can add at least twenty thousand dollars of income *each year* throughout a student's life. In a class of twenty students, this teacher can add four hundred thousand dollars *yearly* to the economy. On the other side of the coin, teachers in the lowest 15 percent can reduce this same amount *yearly* from the economy.

Economic and academic gains were not the only positive effects of excellent teaching. A study conducted with 2.5 million students over a twenty-year period at Columbia and Harvard Universities demonstrated that effective teachers also had an effect on increasing college matriculation and reducing teenage pregnancies (Chetty, Friedman, and Rockoff, 2012).

If an effective teacher has the most significant influence on student learning as well as on other positive influences regardless of the background from which students come, then it is essential to understand what teachers should know and be able to do that contributes to their effectiveness. This information should form the foundation of how teachers are prepared and must be given solid consideration so that they can provide the best education for our students, and therefore, for our nation (Schmidt, 2014). The education of teachers is of such critical importance that, according to Sims (2014), *it is an issue of national security.*

To put it succinctly, if we want to improve education, we must improve the effectiveness of teachers. If we want to improve the effectiveness of teachers, we must improve how they are prepared.

Part I

The Teacher Education Consortium (TEC)

Chapter Four

Designing and Administering the Teacher Education Program

BACKGROUND

The Tenth Amendment to the Constitution gives control of teacher education to the states. Each state has particular requirements for a teacher education program to be registered. As such, the program must follow those requirements.

The program must also flow from the college/university mission statement. This means that the teacher education curriculum must include all components of the mission. If the university states that "service" is part of its mission, then the program includes not only service as one component but reflects all other components as well. Generally, the program accomplishes this by describing the type of teacher the particular college/university desires to develop.

This description is particularly important, because it presents a clear vision of what the university considers to be effective teaching, *focuses on results (outcomes) rather than input*, and serves as one of the bases to guide the program and evaluate whether at its completion, each student can provide solid evidence that s/he has developed into that particular type of teacher.

It is obvious from the above that before any consideration can be given to a particular part of the teacher education curriculum, implementation, or administration, the program must first be derived from the state requirements and the university's mission. There is no flexibility in either of these requirements.

Where there is flexibility is in who determines what the program will look like. To a large degree, it has often been decided solely by the teacher education dean/chair along with the teacher education faculty. Other university participants include program graduates, students currently in the program, liberal arts faculty, college/university administrators, and university union representatives. These university participants bring their unique points of view to the program.

While the university has ultimate responsibility for the program and must take leadership for it, that singular approach is very shortsighted. To have an effective program, anyone who is a stakeholder should have input to create a win-win situation.

Consider the value of the perspectives of the following non-university participants—school district administrators, members of boards of education, cooperating teachers, high school students, parents, union representatives, principals in schools that employ program graduates, members of the community, and businesses. All these people should be involved in program development, maintenance, evaluation, and adjustment. Mission (2014), when describing what the most successful countries in developing teachers do, identifies the following as one of several success factors: "Sustainable, scalable partnerships so that the benefits of close collaboration among schools, education systems, and universities can become widespread."

While school districts and higher education both acknowledge that they have to work together to move the dial on student achievement, a new report recognizes that they are not presently collaborating effectively (Adams, 2014). Though 90% of school superintendents and 80% of university heads say that collaboration between them is extremely or very important, only 33% and 34% respectively say that they are actually collaborating effectively.

Cultural differences, time, and resources are cited as barriers. These barriers can be overcome with fresh and innovative thinking.

The preliminary work, research, and initiative for the creation of this group must originate with the education department in the university. The education department should look into the work done by education innovation clusters, regional partnerships which include school districts, research organizations, and private companies to improve schools (Molnar, 2015). These groups focus on advancing tools, policies, and practices after considering what works and does not work in improving schools, with a focus on digital teaching and learning. Education innovation clusters also offer the potential to pool assets, perspectives, and talents.

Armed with all this research, members of the education department should offer a framework for a proposed collaborative body and present it to local school districts and community leaders with an emphasis on how each will benefit. The framework will be a starting point for the formation of a collaborative effort to improve teacher education for the university, school districts, and the community.

Periodically, this group can meet to discuss reciprocal interests, how the program is evolving, where modifications might be made to have continuous improvement, and what effective professional development can be offered by school districts. An agreed-upon time and place for these meetings can be arranged in advance and be included in the school district and university calendars. Daily communication can also be conducted by email.

The name of the group is not particularly important. What is important is its purpose and function. Therefore, the name of the group should reflect its intent. For the purposes of this book, this collaborative group will be called the Teacher Education Consortium (TEC).

For clarity and consistency, schools/divisions/departments of teacher education will subsequently be referred to as the university, teacher education faculty as education instructors, and teacher education students as candidates with the exception of those who reach the student teaching level. They will be called student teachers.

There is no limit as to what the TEC can accomplish for mutual benefit. Examine just *a few* of the contributions of each of the potential members.

ADMINISTRATORS IN THE DISTRICTS WHERE TEACHER EDUCATION CANDIDATES ARE PLACED FOR FIELD EXPERIENCES, AND IN PARTICULAR, FOR STUDENT TEACHING

Administrators (superintendents, assistant superintendents, principals) communicate to all TEC participants the district expectations. These may be reflected in the contracts that the districts have with unions and/or in expectations and protocols decided upon by the particular boards of education. Some of these could include what is expected of any candidates who are allowed to observe and complete relevant assignments in district classrooms, in particular, during student teaching.

Administrators communicate what their curricula are, what they expect from their teachers, in particular *new* teachers, what their problems are, how these teachers could have been better prepared, what support they have, and what ongoing professional development opportunities are available for *all* teachers.

In many cases, the job descriptions of administrators could be re-examined for review, adjustment, and reorganization. Principals, in particular, have the most to gain and contribute.

The Wallace Foundation has developed a series of five videos for school leaders. The topics include:

- Shaping a vision of academic success for all students
- Creating a climate hospitable to education
- Cultivating leadership in others

- Improving instruction
- Managing people, data, and processes to foster school improvement (Superville, 2015).

Consider how the members of the university can assist with all of the above.

Principals are principal teachers, and more recently, principal learners. They should be able to demonstrate excellent teaching themselves, be aware of best practices, and know how to assist teachers who are not up to par. Above all, principals should support their teachers. These administrators have been encouraged to wander around the building; work closely with peripheral staff generally on the sidelines such as bus drivers, cafeteria workers, or janitors; and build up relationships with the community. All of these activities strengthen the school and the teachers who work within it.

School district administrators are in a particularly advantageous position to help promote diversity in the teaching workforce. It is generally recognized that minority teachers and administrators are needed, especially in minority communities (Goral, 2015). Universities are constantly seeking diverse candidates.

One way districts can feed universities these candidates is to support the establishment of some type of future teachers club for minorities. A main focus of this club would be to draft talented minorities into teaching and enhance their capabilities in passing the teaching license examinations, in particular, the general knowledge component.

Minorities have had consistently lower *average* scores on these examinations than those of their white counterparts (see chapter 5). This situation has limited their ability to secure teaching positions and, in some instances, has discouraged minorities from even considering teaching as a possible occupation. Minorities in future teacher clubs can also audit classes in the university, not only education classes, but others that can boost general knowledge.

In TEC discussions, suggestions are obtained with respect to how to digitally interconnect the school districts with the universities—how school districts and teacher education programs can collaborate to create virtual networks for both candidates and practicing teachers; what networks, especially personal learning networks, can be established; how the structure of the school, the school day, and calendar can be adjusted for mutual benefit; what role teacher education faculty would have in professional development, training cooperating teachers, and conducting collaborative research; and what other contributions the university could make to districts.

In this vein, university faculty in computer science/technology fields can assist school district teachers with implementing technology in their classrooms. These professors can also work with school districts to make sure that their systems are up to par and kept private and cyber secure, thereby safe from hacking.

Recently, professors at the University of North Carolina connected with the state's software giant, SAS, to develop a customizable dashboard that was used to identify problems in how the state educated teachers for its public schools (Stansbury, 2015). Information obtained from the dashboard was not only important for the state but also for other stakeholders such as school districts, legislators, policy makers, and teacher education programs. Data gleaned from the dashboard were divided into four main categories: recruitment and selection, educator preparation, performance and employment, and university-school partnerships.

COOPERATING TEACHERS

These teachers work with and mentor student teachers at the grassroots level. Student teachers spend a full semester in the cooperating teacher's classroom. Through the TEC, cooperating teachers communicate their expectations of student teachers or of any other candidates involved in field work.

Cooperating teachers make known any issues they have had with student teachers that might have been problematic. For example, lack of initiative; inability to present the curriculum adequately, whether this be lack of knowledge, process, or both; or inability to relate to students. Expectations regarding promptness and absences are reinforced. Cooperating teachers share examples of excellence as well as deficiencies observed in student teachers.

Teachers who are not cooperating teachers but have candidates observe and participate in classes before student teaching also have significant input into the program. School district teachers participate in pre-student teaching courses at the university. These teachers also share their experiences with effective principals alerting all participating principals with respect to improvements they can make with their teachers.

The school district administrators and education instructors develop a procedure for selecting cooperating teachers. Since the research consistently indicates that they are most influential in determining the future practice of teacher candidates, cooperating teacher selection must be clear. As integral members of the TEC, cooperating teachers (as well as all teachers in the district) become thoroughly familiar with the university part of the teacher education program. Included in this familiarity are how topics in the university program are operationalized in the cooperating teacher's classroom, which measurable objectives of the student teaching experience would be involved, and how to ensure effective communication between the student teaching supervisor and the cooperating teacher.

The relationship between the cooperating teacher and student teacher should be symbiotic. Cooperating teachers communicate what they can do to be effective with their student teachers and how the student teacher can contribute to the cooperating teacher's classroom and to the school.

Henchey (2011) shares some advice for cooperating teachers after she had her first student teacher.

- Project positive energy but avoid sheltering your student teacher from the realities of teaching.
- Offer support but don't force it—teachers need to learn when and how to ask for help.
- Explain your actions and motivations.
- Help the student teacher to break down the experience, focusing on specific aspects of effective teaching.
- Don't be afraid to admit your shortcomings and welcome feedback and support from your student teacher.

DeWitt (2014) adds his voice in addressing cooperating teachers. He advises them to remember that they were new and young once and that most pre-service teachers are afraid of making a mistake. They need guidance especially when they do things that demonstrate their lack of experience. If the student teacher wants to do something differently, be open because the cooperating teacher could possibly learn something. And avoid treating the student teacher as a "gopher."

HIGH SCHOOL STUDENTS AND PARENTS IN COOPERATING SCHOOL DISTRICTS

High school students reinforce what types of teachers have been effective and what teaching methods have increased or inhibited learning. They can also describe what technological devices are being used and how teachers can take advantage of this knowledge. Parents share experiences that their children have had with teachers who facilitated or hindered learning.

UNION REPRESENTATIVES

Union representatives include those from school districts and from the universities. District union leaders explain some of the main features in their contracts that may be relevant to teacher education programs. These might include possible compensation for cooperating teachers and other teachers involved with the program. Both district and university union representatives discuss time and resources needed for the involvement of teachers and university professors in professional development (see chapter 9).

Problems with finding funding for housing student teachers in areas where districts are far removed from universities or resources for transporting candidates for pre-student teaching field placements can be discussed. Union leaders from universities have input regarding time factors for faculty to be involved with school districts. Union representatives from both school districts and universities could also explain how in addition to protections and compensations for their members, unions are also held accountable.

EDUCATION INSTRUCTORS

Education instructors are reminded of and alerted to the district curriculum and concerns, what expectations pre-student teacher field placement teachers and cooperating teachers have respectively of university candidates and student teachers, and what the district expects from new teachers. This knowledge increases the probability that graduates are prepared for their first years of teaching, and in particular, for their first week.

Education instructors offer to school district personnel the latest verified research regarding teaching practices, identify when these practices should be used, and provide demonstrations that show how to implement them. Education faculty should also have a say in which cooperating teachers will be involved with student teachers. There have been too many examples of cooperating teachers' taking coffee breaks or working on personal business while leaving student teachers unattended in the classroom. Besides being unprofessional, in many states there may also be legal ramifications to leaving an unlicensed person alone with students in a classroom.

COLLEGE/UNIVERSITY ADMINISTRATORS

University deans and department chairs outside of teacher education are exposed to the complexities of the education school/department's involvement with school districts. These complexities can be considered in negotiating schedules of education faculty, and, if necessary, providing any compensation that can be made to school district personnel involved in the teacher education program. Funding sources can also be explored.

Compensations do not necessarily have to be monetary. They can be of a nature that does not cost the university anything. For example, cooperating teachers or members of their immediate families can be awarded a free course. If not used, this free course could also be transferred to any other teacher in the district. This perk is especially attractive to teachers if courses are offered on a graduate level, for in order to accumulate credits for salary increments, courses on the graduate level are usually required.

Cooperating teachers could be listed in the university catalog. They could also be invited to attend free of charge any events on campus and be issued a university identification card for use in the library or other relevant places.

LIBERAL ARTS FACULTY

These university members become more aware of the curriculum for which teacher education students will be responsible in school districts. Liberal arts faculty can then teach this content that future teachers need and contribute to developing the syllabi of methods courses, thus merging content with pedagogical education. These members work with school district teachers to enhance their subject matter knowledge and perspective. Liberal arts faculty play an important role in developing critical thinking skills in candidates (and in all university students and district teachers).

It is highly likely that there is stated in the curriculum goals of any school district in the United States, and perhaps throughout the world, the desire to develop critical thinking in their students. Critical thinking is a staple educational goal that has become a mantra not only for those involved in education but also among business leaders. Since liberal arts professors will be the ones who have the most occasions to focus on critical thinking in different subject areas, some brief comments about critical thinking are in order. These comments are particularly relevant considering the criticism regarding the lack of colleges and universities in promoting critical thinking in their students (see chapter 2).

Critical thinking is the foundation of our communication skills—writing, reading, speaking, and listening. Social change is made possible by critical thinking. Institutions have their own assumptions which must be constantly scrutinized. Our biases can be revealed through critical thinking. This revelation is an important step toward connecting with people different from ourselves. Critical thinking allows us to question whatever we see, hear, and read. Thus it frees us from incomplete truths and deception. Critical thinking allows us to evaluate every situation we confront on a daily basis. In essence, *our quality of life is determined by how we think* because we *are* what we think (Paul & Elder, 2008).

Though there is general agreement that critical thinking should be developed in our students, there is no agreement exactly how to define it. Regardless of the way critical thinking is defined, it is complex. Teachers (and professors) can get bogged down in arguments about its definition. The concept of critical thinking becomes more useful when describing what a critical thinker does. Then questions can be formulated that will elicit those activities.

The attributes of a critical thinker have been described by Ferrett (1997):

- Asks pertinent questions
- Assesses statements and arguments
- Is able to admit a lack of understanding or information
- Has a sense of curiosity
- Is interested in finding new solutions
- Is able to clearly define a set of criteria for analyzing ideas
- Is willing to examine beliefs, assumptions, and opinions and weigh them against facts
- Listens carefully to others and is able to give feedback
- Sees that critical thinking is a lifelong process of self-assessment
- Suspends judgment until all facts have been gathered and considered
- Looks for evidence to support assumptions and beliefs
- Is able to adjust opinions when new facts are found
- Examines problems closely
- Is able to reject information that is incorrect or irrelevant (p. 37)

Students at all levels skilled in critical thinking are thorough. They can distinguish between facts and opinions, ask powerful questions, make detailed observations, define terms, identify assumptions, and make assertions on the basis of sound logic and evidence (Ellis, 2000).

Compare the attributes of a critical thinker (Ferrett, 1997) with those of a well-cultivated critical thinker that follow below:

- Raises vital questions and problems, formulating them clearly and precisely
- Gathers and assesses relevant information, uses abstract ideas to interpret the information effectively, comes to well-reasoned conclusions and solutions, testing them against relevant criteria and standards
- Thinks open-mindedly within alternative systems of thought, recognizing and assessing, as need be, their assumptions, implications, and practical consequences
- Communicates effectively with others in figuring out solutions to complex problems

Critical thinking is, in short, self-directed, self-disciplined, self-monitored, and self-corrective thinking. It presupposes assent to rigorous standards of excellence and mindful command of their use. It entails effective communication and problem-solving abilities and a commitment to overcome our native egocentrism and sociocentrism (Paul & Elder, 2008).

It is obvious from all of the above that critical thinking is a formidable task. It requires that professors and teachers be able to think critically themselves so that they will be in a better position to develop the critical thinking process in their students.

One of the reasons that critical thinking is so elusive is that humans are dominated by a tendency to think and feel egocentrically. When people believe uncritically what they were taught to believe, they unconsciously use egocentric standards to justify their beliefs (Paul & Elder, 2001, 2008). These authors offer five attitudes that should be examined to see how thinking serves egocentric agendas and how thoughts can be opened to develop rational fair-mindedness.

1. It is true because *I* believe it. We assume unconsciously that others who agree with us are right and those who do not agree are wrong, egocentrically assuming we have a unique insight into the *truth*.
2. It is true because *we* believe it. We egocentrically assume that the groups to which we are members (friends, country, religion, occupation, etc.) have a unique insight into the *truth*. This situation leads to a "group think" mentality. World War II U.S. General George S. Patton warned, "If everyone is thinking alike, then somebody isn't thinking."
3. It is true because I *want* to believe it. We more readily believe what coincides with what we egocentrically want to believe even to the point of absurdity. (It also follows that I do not believe it because I do not want to believe it.)
4. It is true because I *have always believed it*. We more easily believe what corresponds with long-held beliefs, egocentrically assuming the correctness of our early beliefs.
5. It is true because it is in *my selfish interest* to believe it. We more readily accept those beliefs which coincide with the advancement of our wealth, power, or position, even if they do not correspond to the ethical principles that we say we hold (adapted from Paul & Elder, 2001, pp. 39–40).

In light of the above, as a prerequisite for studying any topic, it is important that liberal arts professors and all professors and teachers analyze their own thinking about that topic and have their developmentally appropriate students analyze their thinking about it according to the above five attitudes.

Critical thinking is not learning how to think but how to think *well* (Nosich, 2009). This means that critical thinking must be *practiced*. "Until thinking skills become overlearned and relatively automatic, they are not likely to be transferred to new situations" (Woolfolk, 2008, p. 338).

BUSINESSES

Business owners and corporations in the community add their voices with respect to the skills new employees have and need when entering the job market. This information, in particular, could affect the liberal arts (core) component of the curriculum which often demands that all college majors require graduates to attain a certain level of computational, writing, and thinking (analytical) skills.

Unfortunately, these skills never seem to be adequately measured, and mere exposure to this need for verification could serve as an impetus for the university to come up with better methodology for teaching these subjects and better determinants of achievement.

In order to accomplish this achievement acquisition, the questions should be: How are students who have completed liberal arts courses different in knowledge from those students who have not taken them? How are students who are liberally educated different in behavior from students who are not liberally educated?

Businesses also offer their own funding or suggestions for funding, methods for increasing efficiency, placements and employment for both non-education and education candidates during the semester and in the summer, and in-/externships for university students who do not choose to be teachers.

Businesses, in particular corporations, can expose universities and school districts to the *thought leadership* that brings cutting-edge ideas and expertise in creating excellence and productivity in any organization. These perspectives can assist universities and districts in analyzing how they function so that they can conduct their activities to increase effectiveness and efficiency.

Education faculty give their input into training and development content and methodology for business employees. Education faculty can offer screening or testing suggestions for business applicants and offer remedial techniques for employees before they can advance to higher levels, or work more efficiently at their present levels.

COMMUNITY REPRESENTATIVES/POLITICIANS

Community representatives and political leaders are exposed to the demands of the university and school districts in providing an excellent teacher education program. Representatives add their perspective into the program along with pressuring federal, state, and local officials to offer whatever support is necessary to ensure an effective teacher education program.

The litany goes on. There is no limit to what this group of TEC members can gain and contribute for the benefit of all.

What is expected is that as a result of all the input in TEC discussions, an agreement should be reached as to the type of teacher the institution should develop, how this can realistically be achieved, who enters the program, what the program will look like, and, especially, how it will be supported, evaluated, and adjusted. Consortium participation should help address the problem that teacher education programs are too theoretical and, thereby, removed from practice, or too vocational, abandoning the theoretical, thus balancing the two (Levine, 2011).

To recapitulate, consider once again the value of having this type of representative consortium, not the least of which is keeping a positive relationship and open communication between the higher education institutions and the school districts where candidates will have field placements as well as possible future employment. This relationship allows education faculty to be aware of what is occurring in school district classrooms and allows field placement teachers and cooperating teachers to be aware of current research and innovative practices as well as what is expected of program candidates.

For example, if the consortium were to develop a flexible lesson plan that would be required of all student teachers, the field teachers and cooperating teachers would immediately have to adjust their teaching to include all the criteria in that lesson plan. This activity would improve education for all the district's students.

Education faculty spend time in district classrooms thus constantly reminding them of the curricula and types of students candidates will have to teach, problems with which teachers must deal on a daily basis such as cultural issues, working with unmotivated students, those with behavior problems, or those who have special needs.

Liberal arts professors are exposed to the content that teaching candidates must communicate along with the types of students with whom candidates must interact. The professors then can adjust their curricula to ensure that this content is reflected in their syllabi. Exposure to different methodologies can help liberal arts professors use some of these techniques to teach relevant content, thus improving their own teaching skills. Liberal arts professors are also predominantly responsible for modeling critical thinking skills and in developing these skills in their students.

School district administrators benefit when their faculty work in conjunction with the university to improve instruction and skills of new and experienced teachers. Parents contribute their perspective concerning how their children are responding to instruction as well as to personal relationships with teachers. Current students in the teacher education program and program graduates provide important insights and feedback regarding what was successful and what was not.

Finally, to ensure that all of the above runs smoothly, a website should be set up for the TEC indicating the official name of the group to be determined by members along with their names and email addresses. This listing allows instant communication among members whenever necessary.

The missions of both the school district(s) and university will be stated on the website along with the type of teacher the university desires to produce. Videos of model lessons taught by student teachers and cooperating teachers will be posted along with all the different coaching rubrics (see chapter 7) that TEC members have developed together. Work completed to demonstrate the achievement of objectives by field placement candidates (pre-student teachers) will also be posted along with any other relevant information.

To allow all TEC members to partake in events offered in the university and school district(s), these events will be listed on the website. To ensure that the contact between the university and the school district(s) is regular and consistent, one person will be appointed from each as a liaison between the two with the responsibility of keeping the website updated monthly.

BLUEPRINT SUMMARY

- University teacher education leaders, prepared in advance with a well-researched tentative teacher education program and plan for working with school districts that emphasizes the mutual benefit for all, initiate contact with these districts and community leaders to establish a TEC.

- TEC representatives from the university include education faculty, liberal arts faculty, university administrators, union representatives, and current and former students. Representatives from school districts include superintendents, principals, subject coordinators, cooperating teachers, other field placement teachers, union representatives, current high school students, and parents. Community representatives include business owners, corporations, public officials, and other community leaders.

- All participants recognize that the TEC is an integral part of developing the skills of both new and practicing teachers in order to promote student achievement.

- All TEC representatives work together to develop a pre-service teacher education program as well as an ongoing meaningful professional development program (see chapter 9) for all teachers who are part of the TEC. Both the teacher education and professional development programs are continually monitored, evaluated, and adjusted, as necessary.

- The TEC will set up its own website indicating membership, showcasing work performed cooperatively, listing events in which members can partake, and posting any other relevant information. An appointed member of the school district and university serves as a liaison to ensure that the website is updated monthly.

Part II

The University Program

Chapter Five

The Teacher Education Candidates

BACKGROUND

There are several routes to the teaching profession. These include following a registered and accredited program at a college/university, taking education courses to meet minimum state certification requirements, completing a master of arts in teaching program, finishing an online degree, or pursuing an alternative route such as Teach for America. This chapter is geared to a discussion of the first route, completing a registered and (hopefully) accredited university program.

Every institution and profession wants top candidates and top employees. School districts, private schools, and universities are no different. Remembering the fact that colleges and universities, public or private, are responsible for the bottom line, it is in the institution's interest to have as many students as feasible. These institutions are subject to the law of supply and demand. Entrance standards become more stringent and selective when more students apply, and become less selective as fewer students apply.

Every department in the university wants students. Large numbers ensure that departments will stay open and that faculty in that department will remain employed.

Admission to the college/university is not necessarily admission to the teacher education program. An important part of the teacher education program is considering whom to admit. The public and the Council for the Accreditation of Educator Preparation (see chapter 1) are demanding that universities be more selective in admitting students into teacher education programs. The challenge is for institutions to develop teachers from diverse backgrounds who will exhibit excellence.

Over the past thirty years, there has been concern over the quality of female candidates entering the teaching profession. One of the reasons is that prior to that time, choices for women were generally geared to the secretarial, nursing, and teaching occupations. But as more opportunities became open to women, the "best and the brightest" began to select law, medicine, accounting, and business programs as opposed to teaching. This situation proved to be a double-edged sword, for while affording more opportunities to women, it left a void of high-quality candidates for teaching. This void does not mean that female teacher education candidates are necessarily weak, only that the pool of higher-level female candidates is smaller.

The reader should not be left with the impression that teacher candidates are intellectually inadequate, for many outstanding students really want to teach and do not pursue other careers. While Auguste, Kihn, and Miller (2010) reported that too many teaching candidates had SAT scores below the fiftieth percentile, more recently, Resmovits (2013) and Lankford et al. (2014) have indicated an increase in academic ability in those entering the profession.

Many reasons are cited by candidates for choosing teaching as a career. These range from wanting to work with young people; contributing to the welfare of the country; being inspired by a former teacher or teachers; wanting to make a difference; social mobility; can't think of anything else to do; summers off; vacations and holidays; an easy job; a good pension; etc. Motivations of candidates have a serious effect on their performance both during the teacher education program and beyond.

CASE IN POINT 7

During the Vietnam War, New York City had a dramatic teacher shortage. The city arranged with the federal government that men who teach there would be exempt from the draft. Many men who desired other occupations took advantage of this opportunity. When it came to registering for education courses needed to meet city certification, most of these men openly stated that they would leave teaching as soon as the war was over.

Meanwhile, the teachers' union negotiated a high salary scale as part of its contract with the city. By the time the Vietnam War was over, these male teachers were earning more money than they would be able to make in jobs in which they were previously more interested. Therefore, many of these teachers remained in the classroom until retirement.

Most institutions do not require their students to declare a major until sophomore year. The question remains whether teacher education candidates have to declare a major other than education or whether the institution allows education itself as a major with a concentration or minor in another curriculum area (see chapter 6).

At the beginning of the first education course, prospective candidates will be given a handbook (manual) that explains *in detail* all the procedures and requirements necessary to enter and continue in the program including student teaching. Careful consideration must be given to the development of this handbook. Candidates should sign a statement that they have received a copy of the handbook and have read the requirements presented in it. If there are any questions regarding any of the procedures, candidates should feel free to ask any of the education faculty for clarification. Members of the Teacher Education Consortium (TEC) would also contribute to and have access to this handbook.

With input from the consortium, the teacher education admission procedure might look something like the following:

An interview is required of prospective students. The interview would be held during a one-week time period during the semester and announced in advance in all relevant documents. This interview could be conducted by the education dean, division director, an education instructor, or a predetermined representative from the TEC.

At the time of the interview, the candidate will have had to achieve a minimum GPA. This GPA is usually 2.7 or 3.0 and will be determined by the TEC as well as by the standard of the accrediting body (Council for the Accreditation of Educator Preparation) for those universities who choose to be accredited. This minimum GPA is stated in both the university catalog and in the education department handbook not only as a requirement for admission to the teacher education program but also for maintaining candidacy.

Students frequently pressure professors for higher grades with the "reasons" that they will not get into a program or lose a scholarship or financial aid. These should never be reasons to give a higher grade. Grades should be based on what that student earned. For clarity and objectivity, criteria for grades should be indicated in course syllabi. Rubrics can help provide this objectivity (see chapters 6 and 7).

Sophomores who are enrolled in their first education course would be eligible to apply for admission to the teacher education program. The advantage of this requirement is that it gives the student some background into the program to see if it fits into a corresponding idea of what teaching involves. It gives the education instructor some insight regarding the potential of the student. Also, sophomores have completed their freshman year in which many of the basic or core courses and grades required for the degree have been completed.

Some of these courses should put the student in a better position for going through the interview, at which time verbal and writing skills are assessed.

And by their second year, candidates will also have accumulated enough credits to have a representative GPA.

Prior to the interview, the candidate is responsible for having three letters of recommendation forwarded to the teacher education department/division attesting to his/her suitability for teaching. These letters could come from former high school teachers, non-education instructors, former or current employers, members of the clergy, or any other *non-relative* who can attest to the character and responsibility level of the student.

During the interview, the teacher candidates present evidence that they have examined their strengths, assets, weakness, and motivations, and have come to a conclusion by reflecting on the following sample survey/questionnaire *or an equivalent* selected by the TEC. The intent of employing the type of document chosen is to provide the prospective candidate with some reflection regarding what effective teaching involves and whether the candidate might be suitable for teaching.

This reflection emphasizes the seriousness of purpose involved in a decision to pursue a teaching career. Whatever the reflection document(s) selected, it would have been presented for examination in the first education course.

SAMPLE: ONE TYPE OF REFLECTIVE DOCUMENT FOR CANDIDATES

When you teach, you do so within an environment. Understanding that environment (context) is critical in helping you to develop your effectiveness.

The context (environment) in which learning takes place involves numerous factors. Among them are you (the teacher), the community in which the school is located, and the students. To be a successful teacher, you should become thoroughly familiar with all of these factors. But the most control you personally have over these factors is yourself.

You are a very important person. *You* are the most critical part of the learning environment, the catalyst that can foster or impede learning. You should be able to capitalize on your strengths and compensate for your weaknesses. But before you can do this, you first have to know what your strengths and weaknesses are.

Socrates said, "Know thyself." Psychologists agree that it is very difficult to know ourselves for we have three faces: the social, personal, and real.

Our social face is our public image: the way we act and how others see us. We can quickly change according to whom we want to impress. We can be "cool" in front of peers and/or try to appear intellectual to our colleagues.

Our personal face is how we perceive ourselves, the person we think we are. We can sometimes exaggerate our assets or judge ourselves too harshly.

Our real face is the true self, the reality which could be seen if we were capable of stripping away all pretense, pride, and self-deception.

Self-diagnosis

> What do you think others think of you?
> What do you think of yourself?
> What differences are there between how you think others see you and how you really are?
> Equally important as knowing what you are is knowing what you are *not*. What are you not?

It has been said that there are three types of people—those who make things happen, those who watch things happen, and those who wonder what happened. In which of these three categories are you?

When promoting his economic issues, former Senator Phil Gramm of Texas would frequently say that there are those who push the wagon and those who ride in the wagon. What he neglected to mention was that there are those who build the wagon. Are you a wagon-builder, a wagon-pusher, or a wagon-rider?

Some Questions for Self-Diagnosis

Are you risk-taker? Some people think that teachers go into the profession because they want secure jobs and are afraid to take risks. Yet risk-taking is important if you want to try new things and be willing to fail, pick up the pieces, and try again. This is the way you will grow as a teacher. Read "To Risk" by William Arthur Ward (n.d.) to see where you stand in this regard.

Well, Are You a Risk-Taker?

Below are other questions to consider for a fuller self-understanding. As you read through them, consider how *each* might impact on your classroom performance.

> What are your values? How do you really know what they are?
> What are your friends' values?
> Who are your heroes, the people you admire?

Attitudes determine behavior. What are your attitudes? How are they demonstrated by your behavior?

WINNING ATTITUDE CHECK

Are you the kind of person who:

Empowers or controls?
Wants to or has to?
Expects success or expects failure?
Celebrates others or complains about others?
Learns from other people or resents others?
Makes commitments or makes promises?
Sees opportunities or sees problems?
Does it or talks about it?
Feels responsible for more than your job or cannot wait to finish your job and leave?
Finds people doing things right or finds them doing things wrong?
Is part of the solution or part of the problem?
Listens or cannot wait to talk?
Works harder than expected or is always too busy?
Takes responsibility or finds excuses?

Are you the kind of person who says:

"Let's find out" or "Nobody knows."
"I'll plan to do that" or "I'll try to do that."
"There should be a better way" or "That's the way it has always been done."
"I was wrong" or "It wasn't my fault."
"If it's going to happen, it's up to me" or "I cannot help it" (adapted from Rinke, 1997).

What is your work ethic?
What evidence can you give to show that you are organized?
What do you do in your leisure time?
What do you know about music and art?
How do you treat people who cannot do anything for you?
How well do you know the subject(s) you are going to teach?
What was the most recent event that caused you to change your mind?
How enthusiastic are you about activities in which you engage?
What evidence can you present to show that you are responsible?
What have you done that shows you are flexible?
How patient are you?
Are you a good listener?
When was the last time you admitted making a mistake?
When was the last time you were able to show your feelings?
Do you have a sense of humor?
How is your self-concept?
Do you make excuses for people including yourself?

Tim Russert (2001), the late host of NBC's *Meet the Press*, said in a commencement address, "Indeed, there is a simple truth, 'No exercise is better for the human heart than reaching down to lift up another.'"

Does it please you to lift someone else up?
On what occasion(s) have you lifted someone else up?

What other questions about teaching or the profession would you ask?
Self-reflection:

- By reflecting honestly on the above questions, you should have identified some of your assets. What are they?
- How will your assets contribute to your teaching?
- What weaknesses did you identify? How might they impede your being effective in the classroom?
- What will you *do* with the results of your self-reflection?

School district administrators in the TEC might use the above or an equivalent sample to distribute to *their teachers* and/or to question themselves. Administrators might add the following to the sample:

Confucius has said, "Choose a job you love, and you will never have to work a day in your life."

Do you love your job?
If so, why?
If not, why?
Why did you go into teaching?

During the interview, the candidate is required to identify the attributes of the teacher the institution wants to develop. This description should be clear to all candidates because it would be listed in the handbook, reviewed at the beginning of each education class, and would appear at the beginning of each education syllabus. The syllabi would also indicate how each particular course contributes to the development of that particular type of teacher (see chapter 6).

The interview assesses the candidate's speech and grammar. Since teachers are important role models, it is imperative that they speak correctly and professionally and not use incorrect grammar in the classroom. The student would be made aware of any grammatical errors in speech during the interview.

Table 5.1 indicates some dos and don'ts recommended by Ryan, Cooper, and Tauer (2008) when using language in the classroom.

Table 5.1. Professional Classroom Speech

Dos	Don'ts
Speak clearly and concisely	Use filler words such as "uh," "like," "you know"
Use gender-neutral terms	Address students as "guys," "you guys," or "fellows"; say instead, "class" or "boys and girls"
Use proper grammar	Use expletives or profanity

(Adapted from Ryan, Cooper, and Tauer, 2008, p. 75.)

When the major part of the interview is completed, the interviewer presents the candidate with the title of an essay from a variety of titles predetermined and periodically revised by the TEC. The candidate completes this essay and gives the document to the interviewer.

The essay is analyzed for organization and mechanics according to the Rubric for Essay Evaluation criteria, Figure 5.1, or a similar rubric selected by the education department/TEC/English faculty. (The criteria described in the rubric would have been introduced, explained, and used in pre-interview writing courses and reinforced in *all* subsequent courses.)

This process is very important because it is commonly accepted that writing correctly is not only for English courses but for all courses. (It is now recognized that all teachers are teachers of writing, and it has been recognized for many years that all teachers are teachers of reading.)

Any errors are underlined and the candidate then has to explain why any of the grammar in or structure of the essay might have been incorrect and, if necessary, repeat the requirement by writing a different essay.

The candidate will have been advised in the handbook that s/he will be expected to sign the National Education Association Code of Ethics (see chapter 1) at the end of the interview. This code will appear in the handbook and will be discussed in the introductory education class. If the candidate is not enrolled in nor has completed an introductory education course in the semester in which the interview is conducted, s/he can request that a member of the education faculty discuss this code with him/her.

States require that teacher education candidates pass a license examination. These tests vary from state to state, but most frequently have a general knowledge section, a writing section, a subject matter section relevant to the area of certification sought, and a teaching skills section. In some cases, just knowing that these tests have to be passed eliminates weaker candidates who self-select not to apply for program admission.

Testing poses a dilemma for the university. If candidates have to pass the license examination before being admitted to the program, this would shut out those who could eventually pass. But the university has no way of guar-

I Organization of Essay

   Criteria

Provided underlying thesis or central idea

Developed central idea logically with distinctions among the beginning, middle, and end

Wrote paragraphs coherently

Supplied details to develop central idea

II Mechanics of Essay

   Criteria

Wrote in complete sentences without fragments and run-on sentences

Avoided spelling errors

Avoided capitalization errors

Avoided punctuation errors

Employed consistent verb tenses

Made subjects agree with verbs

Made pronouns agree with nouns

Used parallel construction

Avoided dangling participles

Placed modifiers correctly

Used appropriate subordinating conjunctions

Used person consistently

Avoided misplaced phrases

Figure 5.1.

anteeing passing. There have been numerous cases where candidates have repeated this examination several times and have not passed. It would be immoral to allow a person to complete a teaching degree and not be able to get a license to teach.

The TEC would have to discuss this issue and determine what the testing requirement would be. To avoid litigation, the agreed-upon requirement regarding testing would have to appear in the catalog and in the education department handbook. And if the university decides that candidates can be admitted to the teacher education program without first passing the test, they would have to sign a statement indicating that they fully understand that if they elect to continue in the program, there is the possibility that they could complete a teaching degree without being able to obtain a teaching license.

Universities that require high SAT/ACT scores for admission do not generally have this problem. There is a high positive correlation between these tests and all license examinations.

Students most frequently have a problem passing the general knowledge section. All liberal arts professors would be made aware of this difficulty and recommend courses or adjust their own courses to accommodate for this lack of knowledge. There is too frequently a disconnect between what the candidates learn in liberal arts courses and what is expected on the general knowledge test.

Many candidates also come to the university deficient from their high school courses. To rectify this problem, universities either offer their own test preparation seminars/courses for teaching license examinations or arrange for or refer to an outside agency to present these courses.

It is important to note that in some tests a candidate can fail one part but do well enough on other parts so that a passing grade is achieved. Think about this: Your child's teacher has completely failed the writing part, but passes anyway because s/he has done well on the math and reading sections.

Parents often express their frustration when they receive notes or emails from teachers that contain misspelled words and/or grammatical errors. It makes parents wonder how these teachers can develop literacy skills in their students. This consideration is especially critical now that, as mentioned earlier in this chapter, every student is a language learner, and teachers in *all* subject areas are considered teachers of writing, language, and reading (Ferlazzo, 2015).

Some have argued that candidates be required to take personality tests. Large companies and the Central Intelligence Agency have found these tests to have high predictive value (Gardner, 2015), and 57 percent of companies are currently using them. Gardner believes that the most important reason for teaching candidates to take well-designed personality tests is to consider their reasons for going into the field and whether they are suited for it; if they are not, they could be saving themselves a lot of time, money, and effort.

Many institutions boast that they have 100 percent passing rates on the teaching license exams. On further examination, these institutions require that their candidates pass the test *before* being admitted into the program. This is especially true in master of arts in teaching programs where students enter with a college degree but have not completed a teacher education program on the undergraduate level. (Testing has other ramifications. When several candidates of "equal" ability apply for the same job, it is not infrequent for the school district to use the test scores to make a final candidate selection.)

There is generally no limit to the number of times a candidate can take the license exam. Many who fail the first or several times eventually do pass the test. This occurrence is especially true for students who have high cognitive skills but English is not their first language.

However, there are some who never pass the test. There is some evidence that the test difficulty, along with university entrance requirements mentioned previously, reflects the law of supply and demand. When there is a need for teachers, the test is easier. When there is a glut in the market, the test is more difficult. This is no consolation for parents who want to be sure that their children's teachers have met high criteria regardless of the teacher supply.

The university is also confronted with a diversity dilemma. All institutions want to draw candidates (and eventual teachers) from diverse populations. But this desire poses a challenge for institutions, especially at a time when teacher education programs are being pressured to tighten their entrance requirements.

The Educational Testing Service, supplying its own data as well as data from other testing companies, continues to confirm that overwhelmingly, Hispanic and African-American candidates score significantly below white students on the teacher license examinations. Moreover, these discrepancies are consistent regardless of the socioeconomic background or teacher education program quality in which these students were candidates.

It has been suggested that performance-based methods could be used to assess candidates' knowledge of pedagogy and teaching ability in addition to the license examinations. This balance would remove a barrier to hiring minority teachers (Moore, 2011; Nettles et al., 2011). It would be an understatement to say that there is much controversy regarding this matter.

More recently, a federal judge ruled that an examination for New York prospective teachers was racist and discriminatory claiming that the skills did not represent the job tasks (Harris, 2015). Pass rates on the exam were 54 percent for African-American and Latino candidates and 75 percent for whites. Questions deemed by the judge to be irrelevant for the job included identifying the mathematical principle of a linear relationship when presented with four examples and reading four passages from the Constitution and selecting which was an example of checks and balances. The test also included reading comprehension and the ability to read basic charts and graphs.

The judge ascertained that this Liberal Arts and Sciences Test, a general knowledge test, began with the premise that all New York teachers should demonstrate an understanding of the liberal arts. Her ruling, however, has other implications. Thousands of minorities who failed this test may be eligible for years of back pay in the sum of millions of dollars. Minorities who were able to obtain only substitute teaching positions as a result of their scores on this test could be promoted to having their own classrooms. The Liberal Arts and Sciences Test was used throughout the state, and although the judge's ruling applied to New York City, the test results could trigger additional lawsuits.

Research has indicated that there is a strong correlation between a student's GPA and higher passing scores on the teacher licensing examinations (Sawchuk, 2012). It was recommended that remediation of any deficiencies in the teaching skills and knowledge of minority candidates be implemented early with most of their struggle caused by not mastering skills in pre-kindergarten to grade twelve education.

While it is not possible for any one person to know everything, it is not unreasonable for institutions, parents, and communities to expect that teachers will have a strong understanding of basic subjects and be able to speak and write English correctly.

CASE IN POINT 8

The teachers' union president of a major U.S. city was interviewed on a radio station in that city. She was being challenged by the interviewers because a twenty-seven million dollar program to pay teachers in that city a bonus if their students improved did not result in gains in student performance. When she was challenged, the interview continued like this:

> Union president: You're trying to stick blame.
> Interviewer: Yeah, I am. Because it's tax money that's involved.
> Union president: That was not tax money; that was grant money; that was federal grant money.
> Interviewer: That's tax money!

BACKGROUND CHECKS

It is most disconcerting for a dean, department chair, or school district to receive periodically a list from the state of the names of teachers whose licenses have been revoked. Reasons for license revocation run the gamut from theft to serious sexual misconduct. States take care in making institutions aware of these teachers in the event that they apply for a job.

The question, therefore, another for TEC deliberation, remains whether to have background checks on candidates who apply for admission to the teacher education program. Though it is not likely that many applicants will have a record, it would be advantageous to find any who might have a blemished past that could present the potential to be detrimental to their students. Besides, the National Education Association Code of Ethics includes the following: Shall not assist any entry into the profession of a person known to be unqualified in respect to character, education, or other relevant attribute.

When all data on the candidates have been collected and the interviews are completed, the teacher education faculty and other members of the TEC meet to discuss the candidates. They are informed in writing of the decision. If rejected, the reasons for the rejection are provided. The TEC decides how many times, if any, the candidate can repeat the application process.

There are several intangibles that are involved in the decision. For example, candidates who are very quiet sometimes suddenly "bloom" when in front of their students. Candidates who are very outgoing could become more reticent and/or withdrawn when teaching a class.

Another intangible is "caring," a quality (disposition) that is desired in all service professions. The accrediting body wants caring candidates and teachers and proof from the institutions that their candidates have this trait. But it is difficult to know when candidates are really caring, and even if they seem to be while proceeding through the certification process, whether they will continue to exhibit this trait throughout their careers. And as mentioned in chapter 2, the word "disposition" has its own problem with some indicating that these dispositions are possibly forcing students to adopt those positions in which they do not believe (Leo, 2005).

To summarize, teacher candidates might evaluate themselves with respect to what Sackstein (2015b) offers as the characteristics of an *ideal* teacher:

- Lifelong learners, always looking to improve
- Eager to connect with diverse leaders to continue to improve practice
- Voracious readers, modeling what they expect of their students
- Transparent in their expectations
- Exhibit a good attitude and a growth mindset
- Model mistakes and growing from them
- Comfortable not knowing, but eager to problem solve
- Technology is seamlessly integrated into their practice
- Student learning is of the utmost importance—they don't control, they conduct, facilitate, empower
- Creative and open to trying new things
- A natural relationship builder and a good reader of situations

- Hard working and nurturing
- Responsible

Like the students we teach, good candidates should always be learning. They are looking for ways to connect with thought leaders and are eager to grow as learners themselves.

BLUEPRINT SUMMARY

- Teacher education faculty/administration develop a detailed handbook for candidates explaining all procedures required to complete the program.

- Teacher education candidates apply for admission to the teacher education program in sophomore year.

- The application process includes an interview with a member of the teacher education faculty or a designated member of the TEC.

- In order to qualify for the interview, the candidate has achieved a specified minimum GPA, preferably 3.0, and has three letters of recommendation from persons other than members of the teacher education faculty or family members sent directly to the teacher education department.

- During the interview, the candidate discusses the results of a self-reflective questionnaire.

- The candidate describes the type of teacher the university wishes to produce and indicates how far s/he has come at that point in achieving that description.

- The candidate is evaluated for speech and grammar. Writing and additional grammar skills are evaluated by completing an essay.

- The candidate signs the National Education Association Code of Ethics.

- The education faculty and TEC members make a decision regarding the candidate's eligibility for admission to the teacher education program.

- The candidates are informed in writing of the decision. If denied, reasons will be identified.

- The TEC decides how many more times, if any, a rejected candidate may reapply.

Chapter Six

The Teacher Education Curriculum

BACKGROUND

There are many different definitions for curriculum. Some include instruction. For the purpose of this book, curriculum will indicate *what* is taught in the teacher education program and instruction will indicate *how* that content is taught. Curriculum and instruction are inextricably linked but they will be discussed in separate chapters.

In our blueprint, the curriculum for all teacher education candidates will have a strong liberal arts component and a major *other than education*. (As stated in chapter 4, liberal arts professors will have to determine how those who take liberal arts courses are different in knowledge and behavior from those who do not.) Even though teachers continue to learn subjects while preparing to teach them, it is crucial that pre-service teachers enter the profession with solid content knowledge upon which they can build.

Teacher education candidates in secondary education will major in the subject they will teach. The major can be a specific subject or the title of the certificate in the particular state in which the degree granting institution is located. For example, a history major can be equivalent to a major in social studies.

Often these majors have ancillary subjects that are required as part of the degree. It is valuable that students take these supportive subjects because in many states, the license to teach one subject allows teachers to teach related subjects. Chemistry students frequently take biology, mathematics, and physics as part of the major requirements, so a chemistry license could allow the teacher to teach all other sciences and even mathematics, if the number of math credits was sufficient for a particular state licensure requirement.

Correspondingly, a license in biology or physics could allow the teacher to teach all other sciences. History (social studies) majors take economics, geography, civics, and other associated courses, and candidates completing this major could be licensed to teach any of these related subjects.

The same holds true for other subjects such as music and art in which, depending on the state, the license covers pre-kindergarten to grade twelve, nursery to grade twelve, or kindergarten to grade twelve. This means that music teachers are licensed to teach general music, chorus, orchestra, and band at all these grade levels. Each of these music areas is a specialty in itself. Imagine a choral teacher having to suddenly teach band without having had any or enough classes in instrumental music and having to deal with students who enter their classes at various levels of performance.

CASE IN POINT 9

Several school districts in Westchester County, New York, had to cut their budgets. As is often the case, music was a subject targeted for cuts. The districts wanted to keep their instrumental programs, so they dismissed the band and orchestra teachers who happened to have had less seniority and were non-tenured and replaced them with general music and chorus teachers who were teaching in the districts longer. This transfer was allowed because the New York State license in music covers general, choral, and instrumental music in grades kindergarten to twelve. Panic followed when the general music and chorus teachers realized that they did not have enough background to teach all the instruments and had just the summer available to get up to par.

Students seeking certification in elementary education will major in one of the main subjects taught in elementary school—English, mathematics, history (social studies), or science. Majors in psychology and sociology will be avoided. Most teacher education instructors will agree that candidates who major in psychology or sociology tend to be weaker and have more difficulty passing the teaching license exams, in particular, the general knowledge section. There is enough anecdotal and empirical evidence to support this perception. The digitally native news outlet for the new global economy, Quartz (2014), in a remarkably consistent report using five different measures from 1946 to 2014, showed that education majors received an average SAT score of 482, psychology majors, 496, and history through physical and mathematical majors from 522.5 to 575. Remember that these are *average* scores so some candidates can score considerably higher (or lower).

There are other reasons why elementary candidates should major in one of the basic subjects taught in the elementary school. Frequently, elementary school teachers plan instruction collaboratively. It is always beneficial to have teachers with one subject strength complement those with another. And teachers with specific subject matter expertise have less difficulty understanding that particular curriculum, even though parts of it may not have been covered in their college classes, and adapting that curriculum to student needs.

Also, having teachers in both elementary and secondary schools with solid subject matter majors should provide these teachers with enough content background to foster the development of this knowledge in students in their classrooms. You will recall from chapter 2 that lack of promoting knowledge as a goal for pre-kindergarten to grade twelve students has been a consistent criticism of teacher education.

It has been suggested that since elementary education candidates teach several subjects, they could have an interdisciplinary major. If this major is to be allowed, it is critically important that it be strong.

EDUCATION COURSES

When examining the catalogs of teacher education programs throughout the country, it becomes evident that these programs are remarkably similar regarding coursework. This persistent pattern usually contains a general arts and sciences component, advanced study in a discipline, a teacher preparation component, and field experience.

More specifically, traditional teacher education programs typically cover foundations of schooling and learning, teaching methods, and student teaching. Foundations of schooling and learning include the areas of educational psychology, educational philosophy/history, and learning principles (theory).

It is noteworthy that this pattern was first put forth in the normal schools (see chapter 1). For the most part, there are four to five of the same textbooks that each of these courses employs. So it appears that the content transmitted through the courses and the textbooks is, essentially, the same.

Before the curriculum is determined, it is the responsibility of the dean/ director/chair of teacher education to exercise leadership so that s/he, the education instructors, and designated members of the Teacher Education Consortium (TEC) conduct *serious comprehensive study* regarding what has been done to improve teacher preparation elsewhere and what is being recommended. This process will help stir the imagination because only what is imagined can produce a bold and creative vision.

If this group is not particularly creative, they can be resourceful. But it is important to indicate that there should not be change for the sake of change, only the type that is truly meaningful.

All information must be up to date. There is nothing more embarrassing than to have an education dean report in a meeting with other education deans that a current "innovation" at his institution is using videos to critique and improve candidates' teaching skills. Videos have been available for these purposes (for those who knew of their existence and were willing to use them) since the 1960s.

Some questions to consider are: What roles will the next generation of teachers play? How will they teach an increasing diverse population? What supportive technological tools will teachers need to help their students function in an interconnected world? How will federal policy now invading the classroom affect teacher creativity, especially for teachers in high poverty schools? What methodologies are subject-specific? What are the mechanics of teaching, some deliberate techniques that can be used in the classroom?

For example, Doug Lemov (2015) found that when he moved about while giving directions such as asking students to take out their homework, he would have to repeat the directions. However, if he stood still while giving directions, the students did it the first time. He learned not to do two things at the same time, in this case, speak while moving.

Another critical question is what are the attributes of an effective teacher, especially as they relate to the university's mission? Stronge (2007) has taken on that question. He identifies traits of great teachers which are fluid and summarized as follows:

- As a person, the teacher cares, demonstrates respect and fairness, interacts positively with learners; is motivated and enthusiastic, and frequently reflects on his/her practice.
- As a classroom manager, the teacher establishes routines, reinforces expectations for positive behavior, anticipates potential problems, interprets and responds to inappropriate behavior immediately, prepares materials in advance, challenges students by balancing novelty and routines, and offers a variety of student learning experiences.
- As an instructional planner, the teacher connects learning activities with objectives, focuses classroom time on teaching and learning, holds students accountable, and takes into consideration students' attention spans and learning styles.
- When implementing instruction, the teacher uses a variety of techniques and instructional strategies, matches instruction to student needs, sets high expectations for achievement and improvement, provides clear examples, and offers guided practice.
- When monitoring student progress, the teacher understands individual student ability, needs, learning styles, and level of achievement; monitors and assesses student progress; uses data to make informed instructional decisions; and provides prompt specific feedback.

Other studies on effective teaching reported by Sparks (2012) suggested that student (pupil) observations might be the key to determining what works in teaching. Student achievement was compared with their observations of their teachers' employing the "seven Cs" of teaching practice:

- Cares about students;
- Captivates them by showing that learning is relevant;
- Confers with students to show their ideas are welcomed and respected;
- Clarifies lessons so knowledge seems feasible;
- Consolidates knowledge so lessons are connected and integrated;
- Controls behavior so students stay on task; and
- Challenges students to achieve.

Once some of the attributes of an effective teacher have been identified, the next question is what the attributes of an effective teacher education program should be to create that teacher. What should be the content, sequence, and time allotted for the content? What research is there that supports practice? What data are needed to evaluate the program? How should that data be analyzed so that program changes can be made as needed? How can "value added" information, that which examines how (and if) student test scores of program graduates have improved, holding constant factors like family characteristics and poverty level, that can skew scores be used?

How can candidates use student data to move the needle on education results? What will future elementary and secondary schools look like? How can candidates prepare their students for a world that does not yet exist? In particular, how have graduates of particular programs performed in the aggregate to raise their students' scores and what measures should be used to determine this? Are there any other universities with which the teacher education program could partner?

To answer these and other relevant questions, participants must study the work done on teacher preparation by various education associations and professional organizations, and the research reported by relevant periodicals. To make this research manageable, each participant could take one or two sources, summarize the information, and share the results.

Some sources for this information would include but not be limited to the National Council on Teacher Quality; the National Education Association; the American Federation of Teachers; the Center for Teaching Quality; the National Academy of Advanced Teacher Education; the National Board for Professional Teaching Standards; the *Journal of Teacher Education*; the National Center for Education Information; the Alliance for Excellent Education; Educational Evaluation and Policy Analysis; the American Educational Research Association; the Commission on Effective Teachers and Teaching; The New Teacher Project; the Consortium for Policy Research in Education;

the Center for Public Education; the National Research Council; the National Commission on Teaching and America's Future; the National Comprehensive Center for Teaching Qualities and Public Agenda; the Association for Supervision and Curriculum Development; the *Journal of Teacher Education*; *Phi Delta Kappan*; and *Teachers College Record*.

Teacher educators who have been critics of teacher education programs could serve as sources of ideas. Not the least among these critics is Arthur Levine, former president of Teachers College at Columbia University. He is, presently, president of the Woodrow Wilson Academy for Teaching and Learning at the Massachusetts Institute of Technology, where he has been involved in actually designing a program that answers his criticisms (Blumenstyk, 2015a).

Levine notes that the bottom line in teacher education is what candidates should know and be able to do (see chapter 3) and whether candidates have that knowledge and those skills. He claims that teacher education programs are anachronisms, which even if strong, are designed on a national, analog, industrial economy that doesn't work anymore. This economy relies on fixed processes and fixed time. Instead, teacher education programs should be reinvented to reflect the global, digital, and information economy.

Levine is working with thirty-three universities in five states, promoting a competency-based program using hybrid models where candidates can proceed at their own rates with mastery as an outcome. He recommends that universities immediately improve what they now have and then take time to think through restructuring their programs for the global, digital information economy. As policy makers look for solutions, and as more competition comes from non-university providers that offer teacher education programs, universities will have to respond to make sure that their programs are state of the art (Blumenstyk, 2015b).

Input on teacher education programs would also be obtained from program graduates and practicing teachers. Beginning teachers reported that there were many aspects of teaching for which they were unprepared. These included not understanding what was required of a professional; not learning how to teach content; not grasping the essentials of classroom management, especially when teachers complain that education school instructors have an aversion to teaching practical skills (Matthews, 2010); not knowing how to plan for instruction; not knowing how to engage students; and needing to learn how to integrate technology, how to differentiate instruction, and how to use and manage student achievement data (Chesley & Jordan, 2012).

In a roundtable discussion supported by the Center for Teaching Quality, and reported by Link (2012), teachers were asked how they would change teacher preparation. Their responses included prepare pre-service teachers for the tough realities of the classroom and how to learn from mistakes; use mentors for beginning teachers; increase field experiences; encourage prospective teachers to develop their own teaching identity consistent with their own personalities; encourage new teachers to learn more about the school, neighborhood, and community in which they will be working; and attract top candidates.

Research would also take participants to examining curricula and implementation regarded successful at various teaching academies, teacher residency programs, non-traditional programs, and at other universities, *especially those that are similar to their institutions*. These institutions range from small private colleges to large public universities. Institutions whose programs have been identified as "promising" include Arizona State University; Wheaton College; East Carolina University; Alverno College; the University of Central Florida; Bank Street College; Relay Graduate School of Education; and Abilene Christian University.

Each of these universities and programs has attributes that could be incorporated. Other colleges and university programs could also be explored as well as determining how top-performing nations such as Singapore and Finland prepare their teachers. And the work of associations of colleges that prepare teachers such as the Consortium of Excellence in Teacher Education could also be investigated.

To add to the complexity of the above considerations, U.S. Secretary of Education Arne Duncan noted that there are more than 1,400 teacher education schools in the United States in addition to hundreds of alternative paths, and "nobody in this country can tell anybody which one is more effective than the other" (Sanchez & Summers, 2014).

Duncan's opinion is confirmed by Fryshman (2014), who states that we are choking on data but few validated experiments which are difficult to implement due to the many teacher and student variables. Therefore, we should be cautious. Fryshman goes on to say:

> Preparing a teacher is in a certain sense far more challenging than preparing other professionals. For all its variations, the physician's focus on the human body is limited. So is the building studied by the architect and the court of law facing the lawyer. The classroom awaiting the teacher, on the other hand, is almost infinite in its variations. [There are] hundreds or so language groups . . . [there is] race, religion, sex, economic background, and age . . . variations in ability, in social problems—interest, physical and mental changes—the list is unending. In a word, there is no professional preparatory program that can encompass every population, let alone every eventuality.

And Popham (2000), who has written extensively on educational evaluation, has stated that teachers exist who violate every instruction principle while still getting excellent results. It has also been recognized that there are some teachers who follow every recommended instructional principle and remain unsuccessful. Gardner (2014b) concludes that this discrepancy occurs because there is a distinction between the art and science of teaching, and that there is a certain chemistry (good or bad) that exists between teachers and students.

As deans move through unchartered waters, not to be minimized are the strategic challenges they will have to tackle in making substantive changes in their faculties' roles, their workloads, as well as coming up with tactical strategies such as handling operational challenges like securing funding, engaging school districts, and working with university administrators and unions.

For instance, the Gates Foundation has added teacher preparation to its grants. They are most interested in programs that

- Give candidates opportunities to master competencies and receive feedback;
- Use information about candidate performance to inform programming;
- Work to respond to hiring districts' needs; and
- Ensure they produce effective teachers (Sawchuk, 2015c).

All of the above mind-boggling considerations will need substantive discussion and preparatory work. The TEC should have significant input into determining the curriculum, while keeping in mind that the degree-granting institution must exercise initiative and leadership in planning and implementing the curriculum and is ultimately responsible for it.

The vital question is what knowledge and skills candidates will need to be ready to teach on day one. The Council for the Accreditation of Educator Preparation and edTPA standards should also be considered whether or not the institution is planning to embrace accreditation and standards-based assessments.

Most skills take a long time and a lot of practice to achieve. Therefore, an important decision to be made is what topics and skills pre-service students should master within the time frame and credit or unit structure for completing the degree and the program.

When should questioning skills, most difficult to master, be taught? Would it be in a general or specific methods course? When should classroom management, a subject even experienced teachers find daunting, be included? Should classroom management be a separate course or part of a methods course? What about learning how students develop, how to diagnose students, identify students with exceptions, and how to prepare instruction for them? What materials should be incorporated into coursework? And when would candidates learn how to differentiate instruction for all students? What repertoire of teaching strategies should the candidates be able to demonstrate?

How will students learn about current technology as it relates to the classroom? What apps are available to help improve candidates' performance and/or improve instruction and evaluation of their students? What could be the role of avatars in helping candidates develop certain skills? How can candidates be prepared for different learning environments—regular classroom interaction, blended learning, and virtual classrooms?

How will the curriculum reflect the shape of higher education in the future? Which specific competencies should be mastered before student teaching? What topics and activities will be included in the student teaching seminar? What should the exit criteria (outcomes) be as they are connected to the type of teacher the university wants to develop?

To confront the challenges of all these monumental considerations, in many cases it would be advantageous to eliminate the curriculum as it currently exists and replace it with fresh thinking. Starting from scratch could be traumatic for many involved education departments and instructors. It would cause a lot of discomfort and frustration along with the usual excuses—lack of time, resources, money, and staff. But discomfort is often needed to propel instructors to reconsider the teacher education program to make it more innovative and contemporary.

For example, instead of offering individual courses, the courses could be arranged in themes. Courses could be integrated or offered separately. A course such as Methods of Teaching Science in the Elementary School could be offered by itself or with elementary mathematics. Courses in Reading and Language Arts could be offered individually or together. An elementary school theme could incorporate all subjects taught in the elementary school.

Some courses could be eliminated altogether and replaced with those that are more creative. Possibilities are limited only by preconceived mindsets. It follows that a final decision would have to be made regarding the number of credits assigned to each course and the total number of credits the program would need, considering realistically other requirements the candidates have to meet to complete the degree.

In other cases, it may be decided that the curriculum may be strong enough as it currently stands so that some minor adjustments can be made. Consider an introductory course, Issues in Education. When examining the syllabus of this course, it may be more beneficial to place the course at the end of the program, when students have had enough experiential background to understand educational issues more fully, and, therefore, take a more enlightened stand on them.

The same holds true for institutions that offer introductory/foundation courses in history and/or philosophy of education. Students who come to these courses at the end of a program when there has been a greater exposure to pre-kindergarten through grade twelve schools enter the courses with a different perspective from that they would have had in the beginning.

Whether the program is revamped completely or merely adjusted, all routines and procedures must also be re-examined to see which, if any, can be improved. Are the program's admission requirements satisfactory? Are the rubrics used reflective of best practices? Are all forms, including those used for advisement, up to date? What advisement procedures could be revamped? What materials should be eliminated or added? What would be the new budgetary needs? Could students begin education classes in freshman year? Which courses should be prerequisites for others? What would be the ideal course sequence? Is there adequate secretarial help and transportation for students?

Regardless of the initial decision regarding coursework, routines, and procedures, the goals and objectives of each course must be mapped out and compared to ensure that there are no significant gaps and no course overlapping. The only exception to the overlapping provision would occur when a repeated objective in a different course is designed to promote deeper understanding or performance at a higher level. As a result of these analyses, adjustments can be made within the parameters of allowed credits.

Concurrent with all these decisions, all participants should take another look at productive ways of organizing candidates. Will the program offer individualized instruction in some parts where candidates can work at their own pace? This choice would imply that much of the coursework would be offered online and/or with blended learning, permitting candidates to complete requirements at different times.

Could the candidates be organized in peer groups (cohorts) of no more than ten where they work together to complete course objectives, monitor each other, and provide feedback? This type of group could sow the seeds for transferring peer relationships to the first year of teaching, setting the stage for working in professional learning communities and the collaboration involved, which has been found to be one of the most critical attributes of professional development programs (see chapter 9).

Yet another decision would involve whether to offer a competency (performance)-based program. Could content be taught through modules? What simulations could be offered? These types of curricula would allow candidates to move through course objectives as they demonstrate the ability to perform them as opposed to spending a pre-ordained amount of seat time in a university classroom. And will the program reflect all of the above?

After an initial curriculum is decided upon, it is not etched in stone. The curriculum can always be adjusted. But at this point a pressing problem would involve candidates caught in the middle of the transition from an old to a new program. How would they be accommodated?

Yet another consideration would be the type of setup that could be put together to keep the teacher education faculty in contact with each other to improve their knowledge and teaching skills. Of tantamount importance, what could the teacher education faculty do to assist in the professional development and teaching skills of non-education faculty?

A topic that would be important at the beginning of any teacher education program is one that develops the understanding of what it is to be a professional and the value in joining professional organizations as student affiliates. Candidates must be made aware of organizations that promote teacher knowledge and growth such as the Association for Supervision and Curriculum Development and the relevant subject specialty groups of the National Education Association. As student-affiliate members, they are kept apprised of new books, materials, and conferences that are held periodically. Candidates can attend these conferences, view exhibits, and participate in lectures and seminars that keep teachers current.

CASE IN POINT 10

A professor whose specialty was classroom management was recruited to present a seminar on that topic for a group of twenty-seven educators. When the professor explained how to complete a coaching rubric using the professional development rubric as an example (see chapter 9), the participants noted that one of the criteria was, "Identified a relevant professional association (or associations)." The participants looked puzzled. Despite the fact that the group represented from three to twenty-six years of teaching experience, only two had heard of a professional organization and those two were guidance counselors. However, all twenty-seven participants belonged to the union.

With all the questions about curriculum to be addressed, teacher educators should focus on how all the information they gather can be organized to reflect the following elements: strong content knowledge, strong pedagogy including learning theory and translating that theory into practice, student engagement, and continuous assessment of learning. In particular, teacher educators should concentrate on the results their program achieves incorporating these elements.

A promising and positive development in the recognition that teacher education needs meaningful improvement, especially from within, occurred when a group of twenty-four deans of schools of education met and organized in 2015 as Deans for Impact. They have committed to four basic principles and are encouraging other teacher education deans throughout the country to do likewise. These principles are: making changes in programs that are data driven; providing common outcome measures; seeking empirically driven validation of teacher preparation methods; and accountability for student learning.

The deans have offered six key questions about learning:

1. How do students understand new ideas?
2. How do students learn and retain new information?
3. How do students solve problems?
4. How does learning transfer to new situations in or outside of the classroom?
5. What motivates children to learn?
6. What are common misconceptions about how students think and learn?

The answers to these questions should be guided by what is currently known about basic cognitive principles. For example, one of the answers to question 1 above is the cognitive principle that students learn new ideas by reference to ideas they already know (Deans for Impact (2015).

Education methods courses should be based on scientific consensus with respect to the cognitive principles regarding how students learn. In these methods courses there should be a focus on how prospective (and practicing) teachers can apply these cognitive principles in the classroom (www.deansforimpact.org). Following through with the prior example, teacher candidates would learn how to determine students' prior knowledge and then design a meaningful way to link that knowledge with new content.

The deans acknowledge that one of the major challenges in implementing courses was changing the beliefs and habits of their tenured education faculty (Pondiscio & Stringer, 2015). This change will require leadership.

EDUCATION COURSE SYLLABI

Beginning with the first education course, a file is set up for each candidate. The purpose of the file is to collect data that document the candidate's achievement of course objectives. These data could include paper and pencil tests, unit and lesson plans constructed (and reconstructed), the results of peer observations, and any other material that shows attainment of objectives. The files are collected to form a portfolio that will be completed during student teaching demonstrating candidate development and growth.

It has often been demonstrated that teachers tend to teach the way they were taught. So whatever the TEC decides regarding the education courses and how they are organized, their syllabi should model the type of instruction teacher education candidates should display when they have their own classrooms. The more exposure students get to well-planned syllabi, the more this planning skill will be transferred to their own teaching. Every course will have a technology component.

At the head of each syllabus, which usually states the course title, its number, credits, and instructor, is a repeat of the description of the teacher that the institution wishes to advance and how that particular course contributes to this advancement. Candidates, in their admission interviews (see chapter 5), will be asked to provide this description and decide at that point where they are in achieving the goal. Periodically, candidates will continue to determine where they are in this regard.

Repeated exposure to this description is important, for many candidates, after graduating from a particular college/university, are clueless with respect to what the mission of the institution is and, in particular, the type of teacher they should be and how it may be different from that of those graduating from other institutions. Repeating this description at the top of each syllabus also reminds instructors and other members of the TEC what their collective goal is to help them stay focused.

All instructors who teach the same course, including adjuncts and selected instructors who do not teach that course, will have input into planning the syllabus. When many different perspectives are involved, there is a better opportunity for the most meaningful objectives to be identified and for activities and materials to be more diverse, engaging, and creative.

All instructors who teach the same course will use the same syllabus. This syllabus would also be required of any adjuncts who teach that course to ensure that all students cover the same content. It has been a frequent criticism that adjuncts and even full-time instructors themselves like to "do their own thing" in courses. This can lead to gaps in knowledge, practice, and course interconnectedness. However, assuming that all the objectives have been addressed and achieved, some time could be allotted in the syllabi for an instructor to add some personal touches.

Syllabi will reflect the best practices of unit planning, the results of solid empirical evidence about teaching and learning. The difference in the way goals and objectives are written in the syllabus should be clear. Goals are statements achievable over the long term, for our purposes, by the end of the semester. Objectives, referred to synonymously in the literature as behavioral, performance, or instructional objectives, are achievable over a short term, for our purposes, at the end of a class period.

It should be noted that objectives must be written correctly—observable, student oriented, and outcome oriented. Goals and objectives should represent several levels of the cognitive (knowledge), affective (attitudes, values, interests), and psychomotor (creative and inventive) domains.

CASE IN POINT 11

An education instructor presented candidates with a list of observable verbs that could be used when writing a behavioral objective. These included but were not limited to state, compose, analyze, identify, list, demonstrate, explain, and define.

She also presented other verbs that were not observable, those considered "no-no's" when writing objectives. These verbs included know, understand, grasp the meaning of, see, believe, realize, and learn. She made the point that students had to do something observable (the first set of verbs) to show that they knew, understood, grasped the meaning of, saw, realized, etc. However, in her course syllabus she offered as an objective, "demonstrate the understanding of." Even though it includes the word "demonstrate," which is observable, this statement essentially means know or understand and is not observable. It is completely different from "demonstrate the process of turning a liquid into a gas."

ASSESSMENT

Current thinking in the public schools promotes the practice that assessment is such an integral part of curriculum and instruction that teachers should first determine how to assess and evaluate what the students will learn (goals and objectives) before planning the actual instruction. Ed Koch, the late former mayor of New York City, would constantly travel around all its five boroughs asking the question, "How am I doing?" He wanted feedback so that he could make changes in what he was doing before it was too late.

Assessment in education has the same function. Assessment:

1. is the process of gathering information on student performance in order to make informed instructional decisions;
2. is used to promote learning by providing teachers with constant feedback on the effectiveness of their instruction; and
3. serves as a rudder for instruction because if the instruction is not working, the teacher must adjust instruction (change course) to ensure student achievement by doing something *different* (Stiggens, 2002, 2005).

Assessment is just as essential for students (and candidates). It makes learning more efficient by concentrating their attention on what is important and encourages student self-monitoring and self-evaluation using clear and impartial criteria. Assessment also promotes motivation by informing students of their achievement. Studies have shown that when assessment is a regular and frequent part of classroom procedures and the students are aware of their progress along the way, student achievement is higher (Bangert-Drowns, Kulik, and Kulik, 1991; Kika, McLaughlin, and Dixon, 1992).

With this focus on assessment in mind, after the goals in the university education syllabi are stated, the syllabi are then created in a backward design containing three columns. The first column lists the objectives, the second column how the objective will be assessed (keeping in mind that one assessment can cover more than one objective), and the third column identifies the instructional activity the student should engage in to meet the objective.

The assessment column in the syllabi is extremely important. Designing ongoing *high-level assessments* in advance facilitates delivery of instruction that will meet the assessments thus giving teachers (in this case, candidates) the mindset to keep them concentrated on the key to successful instruction—student achievement. Seeing this model often enough makes it easier for candidates to transfer this focus on assessment to their future work in the classroom.

When appropriate, a variety of activities are available for candidates to be able to demonstrate the assessment to show that the objective has been achieved. The three-column structure allows education instructors to more readily note the types of activities they are offering. Instructors are constantly asking which activities will best assist the candidates in performing the assessments. Frequently, the answer to that question will come from the candidates, especially if instructors ask them which activities would best help their learning.

Once again, constant exposure to this backward design allows candidates to be better equipped to transfer this model into their own teaching. This design enables both the education instructors and candidates to look at appropriate and relevant high-level assessments and what best activities should be employed to perform the assessments.

Attention must be given to materials that will be used with instructional activities. Materials should be hands-on when appropriate, incorporate several senses, and include when relevant, primary sources.

In methods and other relevant courses, it would be most valuable for instructors to expose teacher education candidates to work samples of students in school districts. These should range from poor to excellent. With the cooperation of the TEC, candidates could collect samples from field placements. Of course, all samples would remain anonymous, but they would provide candidates with the opportunity to engage in diagnostic teaching, in particular for students in public schools having difficulty. Candidates would learn to perform error analyses to decide if the original instruction provided students was adequate, and if not, what instruction could have been more effective, and what appropriate remediation would be necessary.

EVALUATION

Evaluation is the process of making a judgment on or assigning a value to student performance such as assigning a grade once the information has been gathered through assessments. When evaluating candidate performance at the *end* of a course, if the instructor decides to include a paper and pencil test

Example:

Table 6.1.

Objective(s)	Assessment	Activities
Write behavioral (instructional, performance) objectives at all levels of the cognitive (knowledge) domain.	Construct a set of cognitive behavioral objectives on the topic, the Constitution, or a topic of choice approved by the instructor. Design a cognitive objective matrix on the Civil War.	Candidates: write behavioral objectives on the Civil War (a topic with which most are familiar); discuss with instructor the handout on Bloom's taxonomy in the cognitive domain or examine The Bloom Construction Wheel; analyze pre-written objectives written by candidates on the Civil War to see what cognitive levels they represent; compare their objectives on the Civil War with those of other candidates; and rewrite their objectives to reflect higher levels of the cognitive domain.

as a final examination, it should demonstrate all the attributes of valid test construction. To have validity, the test should reflect *all* objectives and provide the number of questions that *correspond to the time the content of those questions was covered in class*. The test should model appropriate test construction practices for short answer and essay questions (Pagliaro, 2012).

If the education instructor decides to give a performance task (produce a product) as part of, in lieu of, or in addition to a final written examination, then the performance is of a high level and demonstrates the achievement of all objectives. The candidates are offered choices in selecting the performance task that would best exemplify their mastery of the content.

It would be in the best interests of all if scoring rubrics were developed with student input *before* candidates engage in any performance tasks (products). Scoring rubrics are a set of criteria for *judging* performance. They list a set of criteria at several levels. In a scoring rubric, the criteria are arranged in a hierarchy that ranges from the poorest to the best performance expressed as standards of achievement.

Example: In a rubric for map legends, the following scores (1, 2, or 3) represent the corresponding performance levels.

Level 3 (higher order): creates an original legend to communicate spatial arrangements and directions
Level 2 (complex): interprets map subtleties that go beyond just reading the legend
Level 1 (basic): states literal meanings of legend items (adapted from Lazear, 1998, p. 56)

It is more effective to write an *even* number of criteria, because when teachers in schools or instructors at the university level judge, respectively, the performance of students or candidates, there is a tendency to judge most performance in the center. In the above example, selected to illustrate the point, most judges would tend to gravitate to level 2.

Before teacher education candidates implement any performance task, it is essential that several examples of outstanding performance tasks be provided. For purposes of comparison and analysis, the instructor also provides candidates with examples of lesser quality products. This exposure makes it easier for candidates to construct the extremes in the scoring rubric before completing those in between.

Included in the final course evaluation is a self-evaluation by the instructor, self-evaluation on the part of the candidate, and candidate evaluation of the instructor. Candidate input could include how they perceived the course goals and objectives, and recommend any improvements and changes that could allow these objectives to be achieved more effectively. Evaluations by candidates are provided anonymously and would be sent directly to the academic dean's office for perusal before being sent back to the individual instructor. This provision would ensure that all instructors would be accountable, including the department head.

Evaluations of instructors would tend to be more positive if continuous feedback (assessment) regarding the course is obtained throughout the semester. The instructor could then make adjustments along with ways to better meet the candidates' needs.

EDUCATION CLASSES

While education course syllabi are designed to reflect the best corresponding parts of unit planning, classes are designed to reflect the best in lesson planning. Lesson planning is a most critical skill, one that practicing teachers identified earlier in this chapter as one that they were not adequately prepared for in their teacher education programs (Chesley & Jordan, 2012).

According to Schmoker (2011, 2013), for many years the attributes of a well-designed lesson have been marginalized in most schools and replaced largely by an unending litany of mostly unproven innovations, fads, and policy requirements. Schmoker affirms that a well-structured lesson is a game-changing intervention that does more to successfully educate students than anything else. He offers the following characteristics of a well-designed lesson which form the core of effective teaching regardless of how creative or "constuctivist" one wishes to be:

- A carefully stated learning objective, why it is important and how it will be assessed;
- Demonstrating (modeling) explicitly how to be able to perform the thinking and work to achieve the objective and thus perform the assessment;
- Guided practice by having the students apply each demonstrated step;
- Checking for understanding by observing to see how the students are applying each step (formative assessment);
- Adjusting instruction for students having difficulty or having students who are successful work in pairs with those students not achieving;
- Repeating the above cycle until all or most students can complete the lesson's assignment, project, or assessment on their own (independent practice).

Moreover, Schmoker (2013) asserts that these elements are applicable in all disciplines and that in only three years of this highly effective instruction, students gain on the average between 35 and 50 percentile points in achievement. It should also be noted that less structure has been associated with more student self-direction (Barker et al., 2014). However, the authors acknowledge that students in the sample were from the safe and quiet environments of the suburbs and that less structured time might not be applicable in areas that are more impoverished.

It has often been said that if you fail to plan, you plan to fail. Lesson planning must not be taken casually but with a lot of effort and thought, even for experienced teachers. Too often teachers tend to "wing it." Sometimes they can get by with some minimal results but careful planning is essential to maximize student achievement.

Rafe Esquith, the teacher of the year in Los Angeles, when asked what the secret to his teaching success was, stated that it was the result of four words, "There are no shortcuts." This was his way of saying that he did not take the path of least resistance, but planned and implemented everything that was necessary to ensure student success.

Each education instructor lesson (class) is geared to a specific objective or set of related objectives attainable within a class period. The objective(s) lead to one of the course goals expressed in the course syllabus.

An activity or several class activities, when completed, direct the candidates' achievement of the objective(s). Instructional activities are selected to best help achieve the objective. There is an activity to practice the objective. If a specific technique is to be learned, it is modeled by the education instructor and practiced by candidates through role playing. A planned lesson evaluation informs both the candidate and education instructor whether or not the objective has been achieved. The instructor informs candidates with respect to the next objective to be achieved. Candidates are *actively engaged* in the class.

When introduced to particular practices, candidates are advised of their applications within the contexts of different subjects. For example, student interaction would be different in language arts and mathematics. The former may have students interact by evaluating each other's writing; the latter might have students interacting through error analysis.

Any candidate who feels that s/he needs more help indicates this need to the education instructor, who arranges a time during his/her posted office hours to redo the content in a *different* way. If the lesson is structured properly, however, there will generally be no need to have remediation. This parallels the situation in schools where if the teacher plans the lesson effectively, there will be a need for reinforcement, but, generally, no or limited need for remediation.

BLUEPRINT SUMMARY

- The university education dean/chair, education instructors, and designated members of the TEC research the teacher preparation recommendations of professional agencies, "model" university programs, and professional periodicals.

- The program has a strong liberal arts component.

- Candidates major in a subject to be taught. Elementary candidates major in English, science, mathematics, or history (social studies). Secondary candidates major in their license title.

- After a considerable amount of research and study, undertaken primarily by the education dean and education instructors, they and TEC members decide the content of courses, their organization, structure, implementation, and student grouping.

- Education courses and individual classes model best practices. All course syllabi are designed as unit plans and organized in a backward design—

objectives, assessment, activities. Individual classes are designed and implemented as lesson plans.

Chapter Seven

Implementing the Teacher Education Curriculum

BACKGROUND

The best curriculum will not reach its full potential unless it is implemented properly. Keeping in mind once again that students tend to teach the way they were taught, it is necessary for education instructors to implement college courses the way the candidates should implement their classes in public/private schools. This means that lecturing is held to a minimum and candidates are actively involved in meaningful learning, not sitting back taking notes.

Planning and delivery are particularly important in education courses so they do not become, "Do as I say, not as I do." A particular criticism candidates have is that the instructor constantly lectures while telling them not to lecture. So the implementation should be, "Don't tell me; show me."

Education instructors model whatever it is that the candidates should learn so that the learning does not become abstract but instead becomes concrete and internalized. The entire program offers candidates many opportunities to encode examples of excellent teaching.

Teacher education candidates are made aware of the objective(s) of *each class*. The objective(s) are introduced in a creative way to show how to stimulate motivation for students in public/private schools. Perhaps the objective is connected to the one attained in the previous class. Several candidates repeat the objective in their own words. The objective is displayed. Candidates are involved in an activity or activities to acquire the objective, and in an evaluation that determines whether the objective was achieved.

If the education instructor wants to teach effective questioning skills, then these skills are demonstrated in *all* of his/her classes. When teaching how to maximize the use of groups, the candidates are arranged in groups and implement proper group procedures.

When teaching how to promote the learning of concepts, the instructor introduces the lesson by involving the students in a concept attainment lesson and then analyzes how the lesson was conducted. Candidates then design their own concept attainment lessons and present them to their classmates.

When teaching how to construct a valid test, education instructors show how their own tests reflect the criteria for validity. In short, effective teaching practices are presented by education instructors who constantly model and demonstrate those practices.

Teacher education candidates should know how their brains work; therefore, classes should reflect what we know about brain-compatible learning. This means that, when applicable, education instructors prime the brain by employing the following:

- Use novelty (something new) balanced with routines
- Capitalize on candidates' interests and emotions
- Use visuals
- Employ music and art to trigger pathways
- Connect lessons with other courses
- Introduce many hands-on activities with multi-sensory stimulation
- Employ discovery approaches
- Use elaborative rehearsal, when appropriate, by avoiding an emphasis on rote learning
- Introduce patterns and provide options
- Use mnemonics
- Have candidates work with each other
- Ensure that candidates, not the instructor, are doing most of the work
- Have candidates apply what they are learning
- Have candidates teach *successfully* lesson content to other candidates

Neuroscientists make additional recommendations: to help control their learning, teach candidates how their brains work; teach candidates about plasticity, how the brain changes physically during learning; use real-world ideas to help understand difficult concepts; and during the day make time for relaxation and rest (down time) in between activities (Zalaznick, 2015). Then reinforce that candidates should use all of the above brain-compatible learning activities with their own students.

All candidates are expected to participate actively in classes, and education instructors make it a point to ensure that they do. Depending on the content being taught, participation is facilitated when students sit in a circle instead of in rows. To encapsulate, the more exposure teacher education candidates get to quality instruction, the easier it will be for them to transfer this quality to their own students.

To enhance the candidates' knowledge and teaching skills (theory and performance), coaching rubrics are used. Coaching rubrics are guided observation instruments that assist teachers and candidates in acquiring, developing, and evaluating teaching skills.

As opposed to scoring rubrics (see chapter 6) which *judge* performance, coaching rubrics *develop* performance. Examine the Coaching Rubric for Lesson Planning and Implementation in Table 7.1.

Notice that the coaching rubric is divided into two columns: Criteria and Performance Indicators. The column on the left lists specific research-based criteria, also known as descriptors, which represent *mastery* performance. The criteria must be specific and observable enough so that more than one person observing the performance will be able to agree that each criterion had or had not been demonstrated. When used as a coaching device, the rubric defines "the absolute best possible performance" (Wiggins, 1998).

Coaching rubric criteria are not necessarily arranged in a hierarchy, as they are in the scoring rubric, but describe excellence, thereby making it easier to distinguish among poor, mediocre, competent, and outstanding performance. *It must be emphasized that it is not possible or even necessary to perform all the criteria all the time.* But using the coaching rubric does serve as a constant reminder regarding what outstanding performance is and how far a teacher or candidate has come in achieving it.

There is a world of difference between knowing *that* and knowing *how*. To ensure that the research indicated by the Criteria column (theory) is translated into practice, the column on the right in the coaching rubric presents the Performance Indicators. To document performance, the teacher in the public or private school, candidate, and/or other evaluator must in this column put in writing exactly how each criterion was actually implemented, providing specific and appropriate examples.

This documentation will be more focused and precise if the same verb and tense stated in the criterion are also used in the indicator. Criteria (descriptor) verbs are expressed in the past tense as should be the Performance Indicators documenting what the teacher or candidate actually did, not what s/he plans to do.

Inappropriate ways to write the Performance Indicator would be stating what will be done in that category; placing a check mark; writing "Satisfied," "Completed," or an equivalent term next to the corresponding criterion; numerically scoring the criterion; or offering an irrelevant example.

Spaces not filled in identify where performance could be improved, unless an example indicated refers to a negative criterion, one to be eliminated. (Some rubrics identify criteria to be avoided such as "Responded negatively

Table 7.1. Coaching Rubric for Lesson Planning and Implementation

Criteria (Descriptors)	Performance Indicators (Examples)
The teacher analyzed and described students' needs	
GOAL	
flowed from unit's identified standard/benchmark	
OBJECTIVE(S)	
stated appropriately (observable, outcome-based, student-oriented)	
flowed from goal	
ENTRY SKILLS	
expressed in behavioral (performance) terms	
ANTICIPATORY SET	
provided an interesting and engaging hook	
connected content to prior learning	
led into lesson objective that was restated by several students in their own words	
The teacher displayed objective	
explained how objective was connected to students' lives	
SEQUENCE OF OBJECTIVES	
written in behavioral (performance) terms	
listed in sequential order, when sequence was important	
ASSESSMENT	
expressed clearly for each objective (though one assessment may cover several objectives)	
CORRESPONDING INSTRUCTIONAL STRATEGIES	
matched the sequence of objectives and assessment	
employed several senses	

involved students with hands-on activities

provided differentiated options

MATERIALS

included multi-sensory experiences

connected to students' lives

included primary sources, when possible

CLASSROOM ORGANIZATION

met most appropriately the lesson objective and needs of students

MODELING

The teacher
demonstrated the skills (if the objective was a skill)

provided examples or products (if the objective was a concept or set of concepts)

GUIDED PRACTICE

reinforced objective by re-teaching it in several different ways

CLOSURE

demonstrated that the students could *perform* the objective

INDEPENDENT PRACTICE

provided activities that were meaningful to and engaging for students

EVALUATION OF LEARNING

measured the attainment of the lesson objective for each student

FOLLOW-UP LESSON

communicated to class

---

to a student's answer," as it might appear in a coaching rubric involving questioning skills.)

Rubrics can be holistic or analytic (Brookhart, 2004). In a holistic rubric, performance is identified in global terms and rated as an overall impression (excellent, good, fair, poor, achieved, not achieved, yes, no) or scored numerically according to a criterion (descriptor), as in the case of the map legend rubric presented in chapter 6, Table 6.1. For a score to be assigned, all the criteria (descriptors) have to be taken into account *simultaneously*. In the case of analyzing teaching performance, the holistic rubric offers little feedback regarding exactly what makes the rating of the performance excellent, fair, or poor.

In contrast, coaching rubrics are *analytic*, whereby each criterion (descriptor) is evaluated *separately* by identifying specific examples of the criterion. Moreover, when evaluators or observers discuss the examples with the teacher or candidate, suggestions can be offered for better examples that could have been implemented.

Table 7.2 summarizes the correct and incorrect ways to complete coaching rubric performance indicators.

Table 7.2. Completing Performance Indicators for Corresponding Coaching Rubric Criteria

Correct Completion	Incorrect Completion
Use the same verb	Use a different verb
Use the same tense	Write what will be done
Provide a specific detailed example	Provide a general or vague example
Provide a relevant example	Provide an irrelevant example
	Use terms such as "Yes," "Completed," or "Satisfied"
	Place a check mark
	Score numerically

Coaching rubrics should be developed for all the strategies included in the teacher education curriculum. Some of these strategies could include questioning, classroom management, test construction, cooperative learning, and whatever strategies are considered important for candidates to be able to implement. It has been reported that there are many teachers implementing different strategies but not enough teachers who implement these strategies with enough skill to deliver what these interventions are intended to produce (Anderson, 2013).

To rectify this problem, coaching rubrics can be developed initially by education instructors and then have candidates and teachers in the Teacher Education Consortium (TEC) discuss and modify criteria. All involved should be familiar with the research so that they understand why the criteria in the rubric are essential (the theory).

Coaching rubrics empower participants to take control over their performance with constant reminders regarding mastery performance, what they performed, and what could yet be performed. As candidates show growth on the coaching rubrics, this documentation is placed in their files. Evidence of this growth occurs during courses and during student teaching.

In conclusion, coaching rubrics:

- Constantly remind teachers and candidates of mastery performance;
- Internalize mastery performance;
- Analyze present teaching performance;
- Compare present performance to best practices by identifying steps (criteria) that could yet be implemented;
- Serve as tools for acquiring new repertoires of strategies;
- Foster communication and dialogue among colleagues to continually identify strategy criteria;
- Provide a forum for discussing with colleagues more effective examples of criteria;
- Provide a structure for adjusting criteria and for creating new rubrics when a new strategy and/or new research emerges; and
- Evaluate the implementation of the strategy after practice.

Table 7.3 summarizes the difference between scoring and coaching rubrics.

Table 7.3. Rubrics

Scoring	Coaching
Judge performance	Develop performance
Criteria arranged in a hierarchy (performance levels)	Criteria not arranged in a hierarchy
All criteria evaluated together to assign a score (holistic)	Each criterion evaluated separately (analytic)
Score (usually numerical) assigned	Specific and accurate example of criterion must be indicated

Coaching rubrics that take a longer time to implement (longer than a class period) are coded (T). Above all, it must be clear that coaching rubrics are *dynamic*. They are works in progress, guidelines whose criteria should be modified when new research develops. As more studies reveal different criteria for performance excellence and as new and validated strategies are proposed, coaching rubrics should be revised and/or new ones developed.

Also, it is essential to understand that a teacher can demonstrate all the criteria in the rubric and yet be ineffective. The reason is that teaching is more than the sum of its parts. There are always intangibles involved that can contribute to effective or ineffective performance.

TECHNOLOGY

We are in an era where students often come to school more tech-savvy than their teachers. Laptops, tablet computers, smartphones, three-dimensional printers, and cloud services are everywhere. Specialty sources can also be found such as sensor-embedded basketballs that help teach math.

Other resources that reflect twenty-first century technology skills include preparing massive open line courses, MOOCs, and gamification, where game design is used in non-game applications to make academic content more engaging.

Sackstein (2015a) offers apps for teachers. They can share links with their students through Bitly; gather articles and videos, especially important for visual learners, on relevant subjects through Pinterest; check assignments and attendance using Skedula; or provide feedback from different locations to students through Voxer.

Education instructors will need to be aware of the tools that candidates and all students are using. Keeping up with those tools that students use for social networks, assignments in different classes, or for other situations is demanding because it is constantly changing. Candidates themselves must be always keeping up to date with current systems and incorporate them into their university classroom learning as well as in the learning candidates will eventually promote with their students.

Therefore, all education courses should have a state-of-the-art technology component to ensure that candidates are up to speed. The technology component should vary according to each course's goals and objectives.

This is quite a challenge because technology is increasing exponentially. As necessary, education instructors should become skilled in technology in order to keep up with the latest advances as they relate to the classroom. In particular, education instructors and candidates must also learn about the technology of the future.

Whenever a widely accepted method such as blended learning is being promoted in public schools, candidates should be exposed to this experience in one of their education classes by actually undergoing a small section of the course through blended learning or whatever the new promising method is.

A discussion would follow regarding what went well, what problems occurred, and/or what changes could be introduced. In the case of blended learning, some questions might be: Was the video clear? Were there any gaps? Were there enough iPads to go around? Were there any download issues? Was the group discussion following the video exposure productive or were the students in the group involved in idle conversation or other non–topic-related activities? If the latter, how could the teacher better monitor the group activity? This is yet another example of how experiential learning in the college classroom can be transferred to the public/private school classroom.

FIELD PLACEMENTS

One thing about which all involved in teacher education and teachers themselves agree is the importance of clinical experiences. A critical part of the teacher education program is the integration of theory with practice. Theory is important because teachers should not be robotic technicians but professionals who fully understand the underlying principles that inform and guide what they do in the classroom. Teachers should be asking themselves every day *why* they are doing what they are doing in the classroom. Practice assists candidates in implementing the theory, for theory alone is useless except as a mental exercise.

One way to integrate theory with practice has already been described earlier by using coaching rubrics. But transfer of theory into practice will be better accommodated if every course has a corresponding field placement in which candidates are able to demonstrate that they have achieved course objectives in a real-world setting.

A field placement in an introductory course allows the candidate to get some sense of what s/he really feels about teaching. All education candidates can view in action (or lack thereof) philosophical, historical, psychological, and methodological issues and/or applications. The required number of field placement hours are determined in advance and listed on each course syllabus.

Every field placement will be *different*. This variety of exposures allows the candidates to experience several grade levels, subjects, and teachers. Candidates will have to move out of their comfort zones and not be allowed to have field placements or even eventually student teaching in the school district or in any school they attended.

To improve coordination between coursework and the field, teachers from the TEC will take field placement candidates. They will present field teachers with the course syllabus and a contract which the teacher signs stating that s/he has read the course objectives and that they will be able to be implemented within that particular setting. At the beginning of the semester, the candidate presents to the education course instructor the signed contract of the field teacher.

Each week, the field teacher signs a record of hours the candidate attended. At the end of the course, the candidate gives the education course instructor the signed record of field placement attendance. Credit is not awarded to any candidate until field placement hours are completed and verified. All contracts and field placement records are placed in the candidate's file.

Depending on the objectives of the course in which the candidate is registered, the field placement in one of the courses can be in a relevant community service agency as opposed to a classroom. The purpose of this type of field placement would be to familiarize candidates with the students' lives outside the classroom. This experience should expose the candidates to the totality of the students' background including the challenges they face in their everyday lives outside of school. Candidates would have to demonstrate that they, just as in a classroom placement, have achieved the objectives of the course when placed in an agency.

STUDENT TEACHING

Student teaching is universally recognized as the most significant field placement. As such, it will be a full-time full semester experience. (It would be preferable that student teaching be implemented for a full year, but that time frame could interfere with other graduation requirements.)

During student teaching, the candidate completes two levels. Those seeking certification in secondary education will student teach on a lower and higher grade represented in the license, usually middle and high school. Those seeking certification in elementary education will student teach in a lower and upper grade, usually kindergarten to third grade and fourth grade to sixth grade. Lower and upper grade levels for both secondary and elementary candidates are determined by the particular state in which the teacher education institution is located.

By the last week of student teaching at each level (middle and high school for secondary students, and lower and higher grades for elementary), the student teacher must be able to demonstrate that s/he can take over successfully the entire schedule of the cooperating teacher.

The goals and objectives of student teaching are delineated in the department handbook. Before student teaching begins, all candidates meet with their student teaching supervisors. At that time, student teachers are reminded of what it means to be a professional. As representatives of themselves and the university, they are expected to arrive early, attend regularly, dress and speak properly, keep confidential any information regarding students, and implement any assignments given by the cooperating teacher.

Sylvestre (2015) gives advice to student teachers.

1. *Do* introduce yourself to teachers, administrators, and guidance counselors. *Don't* forget to say thank you for the opportunity to partner with that school.
2. *Do* eat lunch in the teacher's lounge and get to know the faculty. *Don't* engage in gossip.

3. *Do* treat this as an opportunity to put your best professional self forward. *Don't* act like you are already an expert. Be gracious about accepting feedback.
4. *Do* stay visible during your student teaching by volunteering for after-school activities. *Don't* focus solely on what you are getting out of the experience; rather think about what added value you can bring to the school.
5. *Do* request informational interviews to obtain job search and resume advice. *Don't* try to catch someone in passing; schedule a meeting at their convenience.
6. *Do* write thank you letters before you leave and continue to stay in touch. *Don't* expect them to remember you if you don't stay in touch.

Student teachers are expected to participate in all relevant activities required of the cooperating teacher. These may include afterschool conferences, other meetings involving colleagues, attendance at conferences, open houses, etc.

Student teachers are also reminded of the protocol regarding complaints with respect to their experience. First the complaint is brought to the attention of the student teaching supervisor. This person discusses and evaluates the complaint. If valid, an adjustment is made regarding the experience. This may mean changing the cooperating teacher, the school, the grade, or any other adjustment deemed legitimate. Note, however, when cooperating teachers are part of the TEC, many of the problems will hardly ever come up.

Student teachers are required to keep a daily log. This log includes the main events of the day reflecting on what went well, what did not, and how the latter could be rectified. The student teaching supervisor, *a full-time member of the university education department* (see chapter 8), periodically goes over the log with the student teacher after each observation.

From the beginning of the student teaching experience, and indicated in meetings with the TEC, there is careful coordination between the student teaching supervisor and the cooperating teacher specifying what the procedures will be for all parties involved. It is critical that the supervisor and cooperating teacher be equals who are on the same wavelength.

The student teacher is formally observed once a week. These observations take place alternately by the cooperating teacher and the student teaching supervisor. Before either gives feedback, the student teacher first gives his/her feedback to see whether s/he can pinpoint positive aspects of performance and what should be changed. Then, depending on who is observing, the supervisor or cooperating teacher gives his/her feedback.

Careful records of the observations of both indicate where the student teacher is strong and where improvement is needed. This improvement is the main focus of subsequent observations so that growth, where it occurs, can be documented. After each observation, the student teacher summarizes in writing what s/he has accomplished, where improvement is still needed, and how s/he will proceed to achieve this growth.

Student teaching should be considered a valuable experience for the cooperating teacher as well as for the supervisor. Many teachers want to be cooperating teachers because they care about students and want to give back to the profession.

The cooperating teacher will have the opportunity to be extremely careful regarding modeling and explaining his/her performance to the student teacher with respect to selecting objectives, materials, and dealing with particular students. Constant communication on these and other topics improve the growth of the cooperating teacher as well as that of the student teacher.

The university supervisor benefits by having constant contact with classroom realities and tapping and testing his/her recommendations for handling instruction, classroom management, and other issues. Observations by the supervisor afford a regular source of examples to help make connections between what is taught in the college classroom and their applications in the public/private school classroom.

It would be valuable for both the supervisor and cooperating teacher to observe once for each student teacher the *same* lesson. The advantage would be in comparing their evaluations to ensure that feedback to the student teacher is consistent. Also, it would give the supervisor and cooperating teacher the opportunity to examine coaching rubric criteria and recommend revisions as necessary.

It would also be beneficial for student teachers placed in the same school to observe each other. Exposure to different lessons and the opportunity to provide feedback tend to improve the performance of all observers.

To assist in improving performance during student teaching, checklists (Table 7.4) commonly used during observations by the cooperating teacher and student teaching supervisor will be *avoided*. Traditionally, observation forms resemble the one presented below, where observers put a check for each competency in the corresponding box. Instead, a lesson plan coaching rubric (see Table 7.1) will be used.

Occasionally, these types of lesson observation forms (Table 7.4) are revised. But they are problematic because receiving a reported rating (score), such as a rating of 3 for Average in any category, while it does give some feedback, does not inform the student teacher during the self-reflective process what "Average" performance actually is nor guide him/her how to improve in that category.

Compare the information communicated to the cooperating teacher, the student teaching supervisor, and the student teacher between the checklist (see Table 7.4) and the coaching rubric (see Table 7.1). Keep in mind that the

Teacher (or Student Teacher)
Grade_____ Date_____ Subject_____

Table 7.4. Lesson Observation

Competencies	1	2	3	4	5	6	7
A personal influence and rapport							
Enthusiasm							
Questioning skill							
Ability to maintain effective discipline							
Ability to motivate learners							
Ability to communicate a definite objective							
Attention to individual needs							
Mastery of subject							
Use of differentiated instructional techniques							
Use of routines							
Fluency in speech							
Creative use of materials							
Skill in achieving broad pupil interaction							
Content/process achieved							
Skill in assessment							

1 – Not achieved
2 – To a limited degree
3 – Average
4 – Strong
5 – Superior
6 – Truly outstanding
7 – No opportunity to observe
COMMENTS: (Use reverse side, if necessary)

Evaluated by_____ Signature of teacher_____

purpose of the observation is to determine current performance status and to provide feedback with respect to how to improve performance.

By comparing the checklist (see Table 7.4), which is one type of scoring rubric, with the analytic coaching rubric (see Table 7.1), it becomes obvious that the checklist does not inform the student teacher how to improve, merely that s/he performed at a certain level on a rating scale. The coaching rubric identifies criteria for excellent performance and provides a space under Performance Indicators where the observer can list specific examples regarding how the criteria were performed.

The coaching rubric also helps the student teacher plan the lesson because the descriptors (Criteria) identify the possible steps that could occur. Blank example (Performance Indicator) spaces tell where the teaching could be improved. Examining the examples performed affords the opportunity for the student teacher and the observer to discuss other examples that could have been employed. (It must be reiterated that no one can be expected to perform all the criteria all the time.)

Coaching rubrics continue to be developed by all interested parties, keeping in mind that the rubrics are dynamic and should be revised, when necessary. Exposure to the coaching rubrics keep cooperating teachers constantly aware of important performance criteria. This contact reminds cooperating teachers how they, as models for their student teachers, should be implementing instruction for the benefit of their own students.

In addition to lesson planning, coaching rubrics can be used to assist student teachers (and cooperating teachers) in developing and evaluating numerous other skills and strategies. Student teachers will have been introduced to many different coaching rubrics in prerequisite education courses. As members of the TEC, cooperating teachers will also have had access to these other coaching rubrics.

It must be mentioned that there are other student teaching models that can be investigated. Care should be taken in selecting any of these models to make sure that they flow seamlessly from the prerequisite part of the program.

For instance, there is a cohort model in which groups (cohorts) of student teachers can work simultaneously in a school rotating through classrooms while learning from several teachers. This model could be effective when candidates did not have the opportunity to be exposed to several different types of classrooms prior to student teaching. But the model may not afford the student teacher the opportunity to get to know the students well enough to plan and evaluate instruction for them over a specified period to see the final result.

The type of student teaching experience should be determined by the goals of the program, input from the TEC, and program graduates. Whatever the decision regarding the type of experience, student teachers should focus on assessment by constantly analyzing learning outcomes and determining what instruction is needed to respond to these outcomes.

THE STUDENT TEACHING SEMINAR

If there is anything that should be said about the student teaching seminar, it is that it should be flexible. Though there are problems and issues common to all student teachers, each group has its own issues.

As in all other courses, the syllabus for the student teaching seminar has a description of the type of teacher the candidate should become and indicates its own goals and objectives. But enough syllabus time should be allotted to listing objectives that the student teachers want to accomplish.

The syllabus is initially prepared by all teacher education faculty, the TEC, and by student teachers themselves. The seminar could include simulated interviews conducted by school district members of the TEC, resume preparation, possible questions student teachers could be asked in job interviews, recurrent problems noted in observations by student teaching supervisors, and guest speakers who are experts on topics deemed to be *pedagogically* important such as technology.

The American Educational Research Association (2013b) has offered some questions that could be included in an interview for a teaching position. These include the following:

- What would your current supervisor say about you?
- Describe the qualities of a highly effective teacher.
- What is the best decision you have ever made?
- Why did you decide to become a teacher?
- Why are you the most qualified applicant for this position?
- Have you ever been fired or asked to leave a position?
- Success in school is proven to be influenced by a child's physical, social, and educational environment. How do these possible contributors influence your classroom?
- Describe the key characteristics of what you consider to be an ideal school.
- What is your favorite aspect of teaching?

The American Educational Research Association (2013b) has also provided a list of factors which *eliminate* teaching candidates from consideration after submitting their cover letters, resumes, and applications.

- Answering questions dishonestly/omitting criminal background violations and misrepresenting certification and licensure qualifications
- Making one generic cover letter submitted for all teaching positions
- Inserting "see resume" when filling out application questions
- Failing to proofread or update job application materials
- Using unprofessional email addresses (e.g., cooldude@gmail.com)
- Going into an interview without first researching the school district(s)
- Submitting resume without including or describing student teaching experience
- Dressing casual for interviews or career fairs (dress-for-success suit is best option)
- Posting inappropriate information on social media
- Including academic buzz words without concrete examples/understanding of concepts
- Failing to follow-up with employers after an interview (send thank you note/email)

School administrators have added their advice for candidates to gain the competitive edge when applying for a teaching position (O'Brien, 2013).

- Make sure the application is update and complete.
- Include key information such as certification, teaching experience, leadership/diverse experience, and technological skills.
- Check for spelling errors.
- Use student-centered language focusing on the impact your actions have on others rather than just stating what you did.
- Be careful with copying and pasting; address documents to the correct district.
- Do your homework in researching the school district and use that knowledge by customizing your cover letter and resume accordingly.
- Tell an authentic, consistent story about your experiences and philosophy as an educator rather than a disconnected brief answer.
- Include field experiences, especially if they are unique.
- Highlight specific experiences, skills, and programs. Avoid generic language and buzz words.
- Positive references from administrators are most valuable.
- Reach out to individuals (friends, family, teachers, and administrators) informing them about your job search. You never know who may be able to help you.

Candidates can also follow a step-by-step plan offered by Leibman (2015) to make their resumes noticed and enhance their employment opportunities.

Some time could be devoted to advising student teachers regarding common mistakes made by first-year teachers. Jackson (2015) has encapsulated common errors: taking everything personally, avoiding dealing with parents, waiting until students were failing to intervene, being afraid to make mistakes, and trying to cover too much content.

Lessons taught that were particularly effective could be discussed along with ways to become familiar with students' strengths and needs. Student teachers should also become aware of what goes on outside the classroom, including the politics involved.

The seminar offers the occasion to revisit and reinforce the issue of professionalism. Discussion follows regarding dress, speech, codes of conduct, and any other relevant topic related to professionalism. Student teachers could also share topics about their districts' standards of professionalism, union contracts, district publications, and board of education meetings.

In addition to feedback during coursework, the seminar is also a time when feedback on the program, including the student teaching seminar itself, should be collected. Student teachers should be able to indicate what their strengths are and where they still need to grow. What should be avoided in the seminar is time devoted to particular certification requirements such as identifying children who may be abused or students who have drug or alcohol problems. Every effort should be made to handle these requirements in another setting.

THE PORTFOLIO

Beginning with their first education course, candidates will have been collecting for their files documentation regarding field placement attendance and implementation of course objectives. At the end of the program, teacher education candidates gather all this material along with that obtained during student teaching to prepare a portfolio to showcase their work, show the results of self-reflection, and document their growth.

The portfolio demonstrates that the candidate has developed into the type of teacher the institution and the department (school of education or division) has stated that they wanted to prepare. If the candidate has not yet achieved some of the criteria for this type of teacher, this will be indicated in the portfolio along with the method(s) the candidate will pursue to achieve the criteria.

The portfolio does not have to be limited to work in education courses. Candidates can place evidence of their knowledge gain in subject matter courses specific to their particular teaching license and in other liberal arts courses.

The portfolio of all candidates also includes a detailed plan illustrating what routines, procedures, and engaging lessons they will implement the first few weeks of school with their own students, adjusting for different grade levels. This plan is extremely important because the lack of thinking through these procedures is responsible for the failure of most beginning teachers and for their ultimately leaving the profession.

The TEC decides what the follow-up on program graduates will be and how it would be implemented. What might a questionnaire a principal has to complete on a candidate look like? What achievement tests will be administered to the candidates' students taking into account value added (see chapter 6) measures? These decisions are communicated to the candidates so that they know in advance how they will be held accountable when they have their own classrooms. The graduates also provide feedback regarding any parts of the program that worked especially well and those which needed improvement.

BLUEPRINT SUMMARY

- Education instructors implement the curriculum by actually modeling what the candidates should be able to do.

- Education instructors develop with other interested parties coaching rubrics for courses to integrate theory and practice.

- A part of each education course is implemented using course-related technology.

- All candidates participate actively in classes.

- Every education course has a field placement in which course objectives are implemented.

- Student teaching is a minimum of a full-time full semester.

- Student teachers complete two levels (middle and high school for secondary and kindergarten to third grade and fourth grade to sixth grade for elementary) and are required at the end of each level to show that they can successfully take over the entire schedule of the cooperating teacher.

- The student teaching seminar is geared to improving instruction and is forward-looking to the beginning of the first week of school.

- During student teaching, additions to candidates' data already accumulated in prior coursework complete a portfolio that documents accomplishments, growth in relevant subject matter content and pedagogy, and readiness to conduct their own class. This documentation includes candidates' evaluations regarding how they have evolved into becoming the type of teacher the university wants to develop and where additional development may be necessary. The portfolio also includes a tentative plan for candidates' possible future students indicating routines, procedures, and lessons for the first week of school.

Chapter Eight

The Teacher Educators

BACKGROUND

As already indicated, curriculum and instruction are critical partners in a teacher education program. They represent the *what* and the *how* of the program. The next consideration is *who* implements the program. Teacher educators include all members of the Teacher Education Consortium (TEC). But this chapter will focus on those who are housed in the university.

EDUCATION INSTRUCTORS

The most solid curriculum and instructional planning is hindered unless taught by effective education instructors. As already specified in chapter 7, these educators must model consistently what they want candidates to learn. This means that they must be competent in whatever they want candidates to do, and if not competent, be willing to learn so that they can become proficient in what they expect from candidates.

No one can know and do everything, so if there is an area that requires special expertise, education instructors should arrange that that expertise be available. This arrangement can be implemented by having a guest give presentations or having demonstrations by videos.

Most states require that candidates have training in recognizing students who have been abused and/or may have drug or alcohol problems. Those who have substantive knowledge in these areas would perform the presentations. New technologies used in schools could be demonstrated by a consultant within or outside of the university.

Teacher education faculty should have an earned PhD or EdD in an area related to the subject they are teaching. The PhD is a research-oriented degree, and having several PhDs on the faculty is particularly useful considering that the teacher education program must reflect the best of the most current research. Arthur Levine, a persistent critic of teacher education who has now offered his own program (see chapter 6), has suggested that the EdD degree "fade away" and be replaced by a degree similar to an MBA as a terminal degree for leadership in the field (Basu, 2012).

A significant criterion for an education instructor is that s/he has attained tenure in a public or private school (preferably public) working successfully with pre-kindergarten to twelfth-grade students. It is not uncommon for universities to hire someone to prepare teachers directly out of a doctoral program without having had any experience working with students in a classroom setting. A report issued in 2006 revealed that 12 percent of education faculty never taught in elementary or secondary schools and that some methods instructors never set foot in a classroom (Green, 2010). There is no doubt that those who have had pre-college classroom experience come to the program with a deeper and more proficient perspective regarding students and their needs, behavior, and performance.

Sometimes a person with a master's degree, whether a full-time faculty member or adjunct, will be teaching education courses. It is necessary that these instructors have had actual successful classroom experience themselves with elementary or secondary students. All adjuncts must follow the syllabi created by the TEC and must be thoroughly familiar with the entire program including all its objectives and procedures. The adjuncts must also fully understand how their course contributes to the curriculum and to the type of teacher the institution wants to develop.

Whether full-time education faculty members have doctoral or master's degrees, salaries for education faculty are generally lower than those of their colleagues in other departments. This situation occurs mainly in large universities and exists even if the education faculty members have nationally recognized names and strong reputations in their field.

It is not uncommon for education departments to hire retired school district personnel (superintendents, assistant superintendents, principals, or teachers) as adjuncts or even full-time faculty. These retirees must understand that their total participation in every phase of the program will be expected.

In almost all institutions, there is a disproportionate number of part-time faculty in all departments. Part-time status is particularly disturbing when it comes to the student teaching supervisor because this person is one of the most important partners in the teacher education program. Graduates of teacher education programs consistently state that student teaching was their most valuable experience.

Yet, in a vast majority of institutions, the selection of the student teaching supervisor is casual, if not cavalier, and frequently a case of convenience.

There are some full-time education instructors who have disdain for student teaching supervision and are satisfied that the department will farm out this responsibility.

It is not unusual for a supervisor to be called in at the last minute to fill the void and be thrust into the process without adequate background and training. This situation is particularly disturbing because the student teaching supervisor should play an integral part in the development of the student teacher and in the program.

Supervisors should be knowledgeable regarding the teacher education program through which student teachers have progressed and work closely with cooperating teachers. Supervisors should constantly concentrate on the description of the type of teacher the institution wants to develop and on the criteria that the student should exhibit in the Coaching Rubric for Lesson Planning (see Table 7.1), as well as on the criteria in coaching rubrics for other strategies.

In the teacher education blueprint, all student teaching supervisors will be full-time education faculty. Some part of their program will be devoted to supervision. This schedule will ensure familiarity with the program and a continuation of the objectives of that program. The involvement of full-time education faculty will keep them in constant contact with the cooperating teachers, school districts, and with the realities of classroom life to ensure that university education courses they teach are current and not abstract. It will also help keep courses focused on practical applications of theory, whether these are selecting appropriate strategies to meet lesson objectives or dealing with classroom management problems.

The education division head sets the tone for professionalism. One question regarding professionalism concerns how education instructors, other college professors, and teachers in public schools should dress. This topic has been debated for years. Education instructors are role models for candidates just as teachers in public/private schools are for students. As such, education instructors should elevate the culture, not emulate it, and know the difference.

Education instructors should use proper speech, grammar, and dress professionally. While clothes may not make a person, they can be major factors in *un*making a person (Wong & Wong, 1998). Research reveals that the clothing worn by teachers affects the work, attitude, and discipline of students. Teachers dress for four main effects:

1. Respect
2. Credibility
3. Acceptance
4. Authority (Wong & Wong, 1998, p. 55)

Teachers often complain that they do not get the respect awarded other professions. Their colleagues retort that those teachers may not be well-groomed and may even speak and behave like the students, making it difficult for *all* teachers to gain public and student respect.

Many teachers have been dressing like their students. This prompted a backlash with school districts which *for teachers* are banning tattoos and piercings, outlawing jeans, and nixing skinny straps (Abutaleb, 2012).

When asked for their advice on dressing, teachers have responded in the following ways (Ferlazzo, 2014):

Dress for coverage
Dress for physical comfort
Dress for savings and efficiency
Dress for a psychological edge

Ferlazzo (2014) shares some relevant comments by teachers:

> It's important to maintain a professional presence as educators and one of the ways we can do that is through what we wear to work. —Rebecca Mieliwocki in *Education Week Teacher*

> When you're dressing for the day as a teacher, always look at your outfit from the students' eye view. —Roxanna Elden in *Education Week Teacher*

> Most Black parents and students here in the Delta still take great offense at teachers who dress too casually in the classroom for it sends the nonverbal message that "What I'm doing here really isn't that important," or worse, "the people for whom I'm doing it aren't really that important. —Renee Moore in *Education Week Teacher*

> You want students and parents to listen to what you have to say, not be distracted by what you are wearing. —Jane Fung in *Education Week Teacher*

Aguilar (2013), in her list of recommendations regarding what to advise new teachers, suggests that they get fashion advice.

> Here's another kind of feedback I want to encourage you to give new teachers: feedback on how they are showing up as professionals. Where I work, many of our new teachers are [twenty-two] years old. Sometimes I notice that they appear dressed as they must have in college, or they're still using their non-teaching-life email address that is inappropriate for a work. I'm increasingly not hesitant to suggest that a new teacher ditch her jeans and sweatshirt and see if that shifts her [ninth] graders respond (*sic*) to her authority. I'm fairly blunt when making these suggestions—and so far, they've been well received. While yes, it would be easier if administrators set dress codes, it's not often that I see those established. But when trying to gain the respect of our students

and their families, it helps if we create a professional environment. I don't suggest stockings and heels, and I know teachers don't have a lot of money to spend on fancy clothes; I suggest a couple of button down shirts and slacks. Okay, this has clearly become a pet peeve of mine (but it's hard not to notice). But finally, and connected to this last rant, I sometimes think about what I wish a coach or mentor had said to me when I started teaching. I had the professional dress down, but I wonder if there were other ways in which I could have shown up more professionally in my interactions with colleagues, parents, or students. Given what I know now, I can easily recall a few things I wish a trusted mentor had brought to my attention.

The point in this discussion is that education instructors model what candidates should wear to impress the importance on candidates as to what they, as professionals, should wear in the classroom. Dressing, as well as implementing courses the way candidates should teach, should not be another "do as I say, not as I do" situation.

LIBERAL ARTS FACULTY

In the case of secondary student teachers, liberal arts professors will observe the student teachers in relevant subject areas in addition to the education instructor. There are many advantages to these observations. They keep the liberal arts professors informed of the content required by the schools. This knowledge transfers into ensuring coverage of this content in college classes. It exposes these professors to the difference between teaching in secondary school and in college and in the considerable difficulty in reaching the former.

THE COOPERATING TEACHER

Research has repeatedly indicated that the cooperating teacher exerts significant influence on the subsequent behavior and teaching style of the student teacher. Yet, this critical role model is often selected by default. Sometimes teachers volunteer to be cooperating teachers when their teaching is less than excellent. Sometimes principals select cooperating teachers on a rotation system or for a myriad of other reasons, none of which being pedagogical. There are situations where union contracts dictate who will be cooperating teachers, especially when compensation is involved.

In our blueprint, the education instructors and the TEC will select the cooperating teachers. The selection is often made after observing the potential cooperating teachers. These teachers will be compensated in some way by the university. Compensation allows greater control over the selection and the process. Principals would have to agree with the selection. Cooperating teachers will be listed in the university catalog.

Cooperating teachers will share *equal status* with education instructors. Cooperating teachers will be trained in the program and will be advised regarding all the coaching rubrics that candidates have received relevant to the student teaching experience. Education instructors will do the training, and, when necessary, show how to implement whatever the cooperating teacher should learn and demonstrate within his/her classroom. This activity keeps cooperating teachers current regarding the latest research with respect to teaching and learning so that they can connect what the student teacher has learned in the college classroom and what s/he is experiencing in the school classroom.

THE PRINCIPAL

An influential member of the TEC and the student teaching team is the school principal. As the principal teacher, s/he should be knowledgeable regarding what teachers should know and be able to do. It is to the principal's advantage and to the school district as a whole to have his/her teachers trained by the education instructors. Cooperating teachers can serve as liaisons between the university and the principals, keeping them informed with respect to best practices. Principals, from their membership in the TEC, will also have had input into what successful student teachers should have learned and be able to perform.

In a majority of cases, the principal, in addition to the college supervisor and cooperating teacher, will also observe the student teacher. This observation will occur once during the semester. The principal gives feedback to the student teacher regarding performance in conjunction with the expectations set forth in the teacher education program objectives. This feedback also includes performance on the indicators listed in the lesson plan coaching rubric whose criteria would have been approved by the TEC. The principal's observation, along with all other observations, will be placed in the student teacher's file.

BLUEPRINT SUMMARY

- Education instructors possess an earned PhD or EdD in an area related to their teaching responsibilities.

- Education instructors have had tenured teaching experience with pre-kindergarten to twelfth-grade students.

- All adjuncts have had tenured teaching experience with pre-kindergarten to twelfth-grade students.

- All adjuncts are thoroughly familiarized with all aspects of the teacher education program.

- All adjuncts follow the syllabi created by the education department/TEC.

- The student teaching supervisor is a *full-time* member of the university teacher education program.

- Liberal arts faculty observe secondary student teachers in subject areas relevant to expertise.

- The education division head sets the tone for teaching excellence and professionalism.

- All education faculty including adjuncts model for candidates proper speech and professional dress.

- Cooperating teachers share equal status with the student teaching supervisor.

- Cooperating teachers receive an agreed upon form of compensation (not necessarily monetary).

- As members of the TEC, cooperating teachers participate in planning the teacher education curriculum, are trained by the education instructors, and are approved by both the principal and the university.

- Whenever possible, the principal observes the student teacher once during the semester and provides feedback on performance.

Part III

Professional Development

Chapter Nine

Effective Professional Development

BACKGROUND

Frances Fuller (1969) spent many years studying the concerns of novice teachers, those in the first several years of practice. She presented empirical evidence that novice teachers passed through a sequence of concern levels, stages of development. Fuller grouped these concern levels into three basic categories: self, task, and impact.

Self. At the self level, teachers are concerned with *survival*. Examples of self level concerns are: Will I be able to control my class? Will the students like me? What will the other teachers in the school think about me? Will I be able to teach content, even within my own discipline, with which I am not familiar? Once these personal concerns are resolved, the teacher is ready to move to the next level, and to do so, teachers need support from colleagues.

Task. At the task level teachers are concerned with *management* of time and job including planning, delivery, and paperwork. Concerns at this level involve: How will I find the time to plan instruction? How can I complete all this paperwork? How can I manage my teaching and personal coursework and responsibilities? What routines should I establish?

Impact. When a teacher reaches the impact level, s/he becomes focused on student *achievement* and on the success of the school itself. Concerns at this level are: Has the student learned the objective? What do I need to improve my teaching? What new strategies can I learn to help the students achieve more? How can I help fellow teachers? How can I contribute to the success of the school's program?

Fuller's research was subsequently verified and expanded by Hall, Wallace, and Dossett (1973) and by Hall and Loucks (1978). All of these researchers have concluded that while a majority of novice teachers reach the task level, some stay at the self level, and *very few ever reach the impact level*. Kimpston (1987) found that teachers who progressed to higher levels of concern were actively involved in continuous staff development. Yet, in a recent Gallup poll it was reported that for first-year teachers, professional engagement is at 35.1 percent; for those teaching between one and three years, 30.9 percent; and it continues to decrease for teachers in their third to fifth years (Heiten, 2013).

We can produce the most qualified candidates who have graduated from teacher education programs that are solid and accredited, have high academic standards, rigorous entry requirements, and provide numerous experiences in schools that are connected to universities. We can produce candidates who are able to employ the most important strategies that research indicates lead to student achievement. But all this knowledge and performance ability of candidates will be ineffective unless as new teachers they are inducted into a profession which fosters meaningful ongoing learning, growth, and development as part of the school culture.

To this day, little of this culture exists, and in most cases, new teachers are often confronted, unfortunately, *with a school culture which reinforces negative practices*. For new teachers to survive and thrive, there must be state-of-the-art professional development to complete their three-part teacher preparation.

CASE IN POINT 12

Linda was student teaching with second grade special education students. She prepared many different materials for them to facilitate learning. The students were involved with and enjoyed her classes and made significant progress. One day, in the faculty lounge, Linda was confronted by three teachers who told her to relax and not knock herself out preparing all the materials. Besides, the teachers said, all the work she was doing made them look bad. Linda went back to campus completely demoralized.

A BRIEF HISTORY OF PROFESSIONAL DEVELOPMENT

The American Association of Colleges for Teacher Education (1976) has identified twelve attributes of a profession. One of these attributes is as follows: "Individual practitioners are characterized by a strong service motivation and lifetime commitment to competence" (p. 12). Yet, throughout the history of teacher education, many researchers have complained that despite many reforms, *little effective change takes place in schools*.

Ravitch (1985), in a report of scholars on major trends in their fields, stated, "If medicine were like education, some doctors would still be bleeding people with leeches" (p. 14). Follow-up research subsequently reported that unbolting the desks was about as far as school reform had gone (Glickman, 1992); that teachers were not using strategies that were developmentally appropriate for learners (Darling-Hammond, 1995); that in Kentucky, new teaching practices were not occurring as a result of introduced reforms (Pipho, 1998); and that instruction that was *easier to implement* was being used rather than that which was pedagogically sound (Baron & Boschee, 1996).

In analyzing why there was little change in teaching practice, Rothman (1997) concluded that successful schools were those that addressed the problem of instructional delivery, and that change in instructional delivery is achieved through carefully planned professional development.

Albert Shanker, the late president of the American Federation of Teachers, is attributed in Marzano (2003) as having said that teaching is not a profession to hang out in. And Schneider (2015) complained that teachers work in a profession that actively thwarts growth.

Professional development is the key to lifelong learning, and the true professional is committed to continued learning. *Teachers who are themselves learners are more successful in developing learning in their students.*

Graduation from any institution is called commencement (beginning). It means that graduation is not the end of what in their university programs teacher education candidates have to learn but has provided the foundation of what they need to continue to learn. Once teaching candidates recognize that graduation is the *beginning* of their development rather than the end, they will avoid burnout and find ahead an exciting and challenging road that will keep them alive throughout their teaching career.

New teachers receive fulfillment when they establish quality relationships with their students and see evidence of their positive achievement. Barth (1990) stated, "Probably nothing within a school has more impact on students in terms of skills development, self-confidence, or classroom behavior than the personal growth of their teachers" (p. 49). Collegiality and professionalism, considered together, was one of the top five school-level factors found to have a significant impact on student achievement (Marzano, 2003).

Prior to the mid-1980s, the typical professional development consisted of "quick-fix" programs. Many of these took the form of afterschool workshops under the heading of in-service training. Most school districts also set aside a day (and a considerable part of their budgets) for professional development, as though a day was sufficient for something as important as improving teacher performance for the growth of students.

Teachers were often offered salary increments after completing a specified number of in-service credits with no follow-up to determine whether content and/or skills presented in the training were acquired and, if so, subsequently applied in the classroom. In addition, professional development decisions were made from the top down, did not take the school context nor individual needs or learning style of the teacher into account, and delivery programs were scheduled inflexibly (Diaz-Maggioli, 2004). It is not difficult to conclude that the results of this type of professional development were very poor.

More recently there has been a shift in preparing teachers from teacher *training* to teacher *education*. This distinction is very important because teacher training presented a one-shot view of teaching that was limited and specific, whereas teacher education presents teaching in a much broader context. Teacher education includes not only pre-service teaching (the education of teachers before they begin to practice), but also in-service teaching for those already practicing. Since no one enters any profession as an expert, this change acknowledges the importance of continued professional development as lifelong learning in teaching.

The impetus for professional development came as a result of Goals 2000 which followed from the National Educational Goals Panel, a group of governors formed after a meeting of governors convened in 1989 by President George H. W. Bush for the purpose of improving academic standards in the schools. Subsequently, President Bill Clinton signed the Goals 2000: Educate America Act (1994) for the purpose of providing funding for eight national goals, building on six offered by the governors. One of the eight goals involves Teacher Education and Professional Development. It stated, "By the year 2000, the nation's teaching force will have access to programs for the continued improvement of their professional skills and the opportunity to acquire the knowledge and skills needed to instruct and prepare all American students for the next century."

The public's demand that teachers be accountable for student learning, a national priority, as evidenced by the Educate America Act (1994), led to less casual and more structured and sophisticated professional development of teachers. Danielson (1996), in the four domains she provided for teaching practices, presented Domain 4: Professional Responsibilities with its emphasis on teachers being committed to students and their learning, thinking systematically about teaching practice, and being members of learning communities.

The National Association of Secondary School Principals (1996) went so far as to suggest that teachers be offered a twelve-month contract so that they would be paid for professional development during the summer. Even though the National Education Association and the American Federation of Teachers, two large teachers' unions, provided their codes of ethics for the profession as a whole, Phelps (1993) offered teachers a voluntary pledge that involved a commitment not only to students and colleagues but also to self-improvement:

1. I will try, at least once, any new approach that seems educationally sound.
2. I will seek the professional opinions of my colleagues on a regular basis.
3. I will share my experiences in the classroom with other educators in a positive manner.
4. I will aim to be a better teacher today than I was yesterday.
5. I will express my appreciation to students, administrators, parents, and peers for the success I have (p. 154).

On January 8, 2002, President George W. Bush signed into law the No Child Left Behind Act of 2001 (NCLB). Two of NCLB's provisions were stronger accountability for results and concentrating resources on proven education methods. In order to align teacher education programs with the high standards for accountability in NCLB, in May 2003, the Ready to Teach Act was introduced in the House of Representatives. At the core of this act is the improvement of the quality of the teaching force by improving preparation of prospective teachers and enhancing professional development activities.

U.S. Secretary of Education Arne Duncan (2011) has complained that despite the intent of Goals 2000, which had as one of its goals the continued improvement of teachers' performance skills, to this day there is not only "lousy professional development, but plenty of it" (p. 70). He states that professional development has become all talk. Duncan points to the fact that the federal government spends 2.5 billion dollars a year on professional development. Unfortunately, this money is often siphoned off into other areas such as purchasing equipment, reducing class size, or hiring more teachers.

In total, *twenty-five billion dollars a year* is spent by the federal government, states, and school districts on teacher development. But teachers still complain that the staff development they receive is a waste of time and has little impact on their teaching. Infusing more money into a system that is not working is pointless.

To complicate the issue, almost 50 percent of new teachers leave within the first five years. Not only is this detrimental to students and districts educationally, but it is also very expensive. The National Commission on Teaching and America's Future (2007) determined that nationwide, the cost of teacher turnover is 7.34 billion dollars a year, which does not take into account the cost of teachers who circulate among schools within the same district looking for better positions.

Teacher turnover costs vary from district to district. The National Commission on Teaching and America's Future reported a range from $4,366 in a rural district, Jemez Valley, to $17,872 in the large city of Chicago. In addition to costs, teacher turnover has a negative effect on student achievement, especially for low-income students (Ronfeldt, Loeb, & Wyckoff, 2012).

Obviously, professional development is not a problem that lacks recognition or funds. The problem would be exacerbated by pouring more money, or even the same funding, into a system that everyone acknowledges does not work. Professional development is a problem that requires serious rethinking and reinvention, both of which should not occur piecemeal but should take place simultaneously.

In a survey conducted by Gallup and reported by Mizell (2013), superintendents in 2,500 school systems responded to a question regarding whether their districts had an effective ongoing professional development for their teachers. Only 30 percent agreed and only 17 percent concurred that there was effective professional development for principals. A few superintendents judged their systems' professional development to be ongoing but not effective or vice versa. Some believed that their programs lacked coherence and targeting. Moreover, this response was despite the fact that there have been for over a decade established standards that describe the policies and practices required for successful professional development and ample resources and money available to have a positive impact on the learning of both teachers and principals.

And in a new study by The New Teacher Project, a non-profit focused on effective teaching, it was determined that professional development needed serious rethinking because what was presently occurring in school districts did not bolster teaching skills and was mainly a waste (Brody, 2015).

EFFECTIVE PROFESSIONAL DEVELOPMENT

In order to fully understand a concept, one must understand not only what it is, but also what it is not. Thomas (2013) offers several ineffective ways to implement professional development:

- Worry more about the time than outcomes.
- Bring in a bevy of consultants.
- Start something new every year without considering progress on or commitment to the previous year's goals.
- Judge quality by the price tag.
- Never listen to your teachers when they tell you what they need.
- Don't participate in the activities you require teachers to attend.
- Take an all-or-nothing approach to conferences and workshops.
- Keep an eye open for the next big thing.

Given all of the above, what can school districts do to deliver *meaningful* professional development? How can teacher effectiveness be strengthened so that there is corresponding change in student growth? What are the evidenced-based practices that should be included in successful professional development?

Professional development has long suffered from an identity crisis. But as professional development has evolved over the past twenty years, less effective traditional approaches have been offered with less frequency. Four main characteristics have now begun to emerge and overtake traditional professional development to make it transformative. The new characteristics are individualization, teacher direction, context, and collaboration. *All four* must be in play in order to be effective. Reflective teaching oversees all of these categories and is so important that it will be addressed separately at the end of this chapter.

Individualization. Just as each individual student has his/her own specific educational needs, so does the teacher. Earlier in this chapter, it was noted that originally, regardless of their status, all teachers took the same type of in-service training offered by school districts. But teachers enter the profession with different skills and need different skill development along with additional abilities as situations change. Some teachers will feel that they need to know more about implementing technology in their classrooms. For example, to connect the classroom experience with the real world of the students, instructional designers at the University of Central Florida presented faculty ongoing mobile technology training courses (Fuhrman, 2015).

Other teachers may believe that they have to hone their planning skills, classroom management skills or both to be able to reach more students. Some may want to acquire knowledge and skills in dealing with the community. Individualization allows teacher learning to be customized.

Teacher-direction. Professional development used to be a one-size-fits-all passive act imposed from the outside. Decisions were made from on high with respect to what development teachers needed. Now teachers must become more involved in their own education and more responsible for determining their own professional development needs. The teacher must continually ask what his/her strengths and weaknesses are, what knowledge and skills will be needed to improve student performance, what new approaches s/he would like to try, and most important, how his/her own learning characteristics are taken into consideration. In many cases, teachers develop their own personal learning plans which are constantly revised to meet the changing needs of both teachers and students. Teacher direction allows the teacher to focus on professional development that is not only more individualized but more growth-driven.

Context. The setting in which learning takes place (the students, the school, and the subject taught) should all be considered when deciding what professional development is needed. Teachers in urban schools have different needs from teachers in rural schools. Teachers who deal with adolescents have different issues from teachers who teach in kindergarten. Those who teach in districts where parents are highly involved in their children's education have different considerations from teachers who are in districts where parents are less engaged. In short, professional development must be designed for subject area, grade level, and type of student.

Collaboration. Teaching used to be a very lonely profession. When teachers closed their doors, they had to fend for themselves with no input from colleagues, only an occasional observation and checklist evaluation from a supervisor or principal. On the occasion of his retirement, John (Jack) Welch (2000), former chief executive officer of General Electric, communicated to his employees that whatever they can do well on their own, they can do much smarter with others.

In this new view of teacher development, every teacher, novice to experienced, no longer practices alone. Being in the open will make all teachers accountable. Each teacher identifies his/her own needs every year, develops a personal learning plan, and is involved in professional development annually.

Every teacher works much smarter by diagnosing students with colleagues, planning together, co-designing and selecting curriculum materials and assessment tools, observing each other, and giving one another feedback regarding performance. Peer interaction has been demonstrated as being necessary for teacher growth (Danielson, 1996). Practicing together helps teachers make that quantum leap between what they know how to do and what they actually do in the classroom.

When providing feedback, there is a focus on clear challenging goals for each teacher, improving student outcomes, attention on individual learning instead of on comparisons with other teachers, mediated feedback from a mentor or other leader in an environment of trust and support, and promoting a professional learning environment that is sustained by the school's leadership (Wright, 2014).

It must be emphasized that merely having a collaborative group is not sufficient. Everyone must understand and implement his/her role in the group. Collaborative teams will have a structure that is specific to the needs of teachers within the team. This structure frequently includes a mentor for groups that have student teachers, interns, or novice teachers. The mentor will be expected to possess expertise or be trained in specific skills relevant to the group's needs.

Some groups will have teacher leaders or be involved with professional learning communities where members, usually teaching the same grade or subject, meet regularly to decide on goals, strategies, and to analyze data. Teacher teams that represent the same subject or grade could instead have peer coaches. "Peer coaching is a confidential process through which two or more professional colleagues work together to reflect on current practices; expand, refine, and build new skills; share ideas; teach one another; conduct classroom research; or solve problems in the workplace. Although peer coaching seems to be the most prominent label for this type of activity, a variety of other names are used in schools: peer support, consulting colleagues, peer sharing, and caring" (Robbins, 2015, p. 17).

There are other kinds of collaborative groups. Troen and Boles (2003) have suggested a collaborative professional development model that offers a *career path* (career ladder or career tier) for teachers that provides corresponding rewards, advanced training, and experiences with parallel pay, responsibilities, supervision, and team management. The career hierarchy for the group includes an instructional aide, teaching intern, associate teacher, teacher, professional teacher, and chief instructor.

Another group, borrowed from Japan, is lesson study, a process where teachers form a team that examines sample lesson plans focusing on what and how to teach. Whatever the type of group, Aguilar (2015) asserts that for a team to be effective, it should know why it exists, create a space for learning, provide healthy conflict, have members who trust each other, and have a facilitator, leader, or shared leaders.

Also relevant to this discussion are the recommendations of the National Network of State Teachers of the Year (2013) to improve the professionalization of teaching:

- Opportunities for career growth that don't require them to leave the classroom;
- Actionable feedback on performance;
- Distributed leadership that gives teachers the ability to mentor, coach, and evaluate peers and contribute to decision making;
- Guiding principles for the profession developed by teachers; and
- Time in schools for collaborative practice.

What matters is clarity in the role of each group member and that the structure of the collaborative group is ascertained by the group's needs. *This requirement may necessitate several types of groups within a school.*

All teams meet regularly and are involved in research to create knowledge rather than just impart information. College instructors who are part of the Teacher Education Consortium (TEC) are involved in planning professional development and in contributing to the teams—liberal arts instructors to subject matter and education instructors to research, theory, and methodology.

To achieve the requirements of all of the above professional development characteristics, a support structure is established to oversee the enterprise. A full-time professional development "czar"/coordinator is appointed for the school district to entrench professional development into the district culture. (For small districts, the coordinator can be part-time.) The label for this person is not important; it is the concept. Universities should offer a program/certificate for this specialized position. The courses will cover *all aspects* of professional development essential to being an effective coordinator.

The coordinator works closely with the TEC and is responsible for ensuring that all new teachers have immediate support; that all of the attributes of effective professional development are being implemented; that every teacher is productively involved; that the collaborative teams have clarity and are appropriate, in place, and functioning effectively; that enough time is afforded all participants; and that there is follow-through to determine the success of the groups in improving teacher performance and student growth. The coordinator also researches and recommends professional development for school leaders (superintendents, assistant superintendents, principals, department heads/chairs).

The coordinator obtains materials and resources, arranges funding (which is ample), appoints assistants in school districts that are very large, seeks feedback from all teachers, evaluates the program yearly, and makes recommendations for improvement. These are likely to necessitate instituting major changes in the school schedule/work week; providing teachers with more time to prepare and collaborate; changing the instructional delivery system; using extracurricular time more creatively; re-allocating resources; and making changes in teacher contract negotiations.

Before proceeding, it would be interesting to compare and contrast the attributes of professional development in teaching described above with those considered vital in any occupation. These attributes have been offered by *Forbes Magazine* (Morrison, 2015). Note which may be the same for teachers and which may be different.

- Duration: effective professional development lasts at least two semesters, and needs a "rhythm" of follow-up and consolidation;
- Targeted: the content should be relevant to the teachers' needs and day-to-day experiences;
- Aligned: no single activity is universally effective—instead it is a combination that reinforced the message from different perspectives that works;
- Content: successful development must consider both subject knowledge and subject-specific teaching techniques;
- Activities: successful development features common types of activities including discussion, experimentation, and analysis and reflection;
- External input: constructive external input provides new perspectives and challenges orthodoxies;
- Collaboration: peer support gives participants an opportunity to work together and refine new approaches;

Table 9.1. A Comparison of Traditional and Current Approaches to Professional Development

Attributes of Traditional Approaches	Attributes of Current Approaches
Same instruction for all	Instruction individualized
Decisions for teacher improvement made by administration	Teacher directed and owned
Lack of support for teacher	Feedback and decisions made collaboratively
Same curriculum for all	Teaching context considered
Delivery system the same for all	Learning style of teacher taken into account
Series of courses with no follow-up	Focus on teacher growth
No evaluation plan	Skills acquired transferred to classroom and evaluated
Different course offerings decided for district as a whole	Continuous follow-up based on results

- Leadership: effective leaders get involved in development, define opportunities, and provide the support needed to embed change.

A FRAMEWORK FOR ACQUIRING TEACHING SKILLS

Whenever a teacher or teams of teachers believes that there is a new skill to be learned or that a prior skill could be improved, they should follow the proven framework for acquiring teaching skills. Achieving even the most basic teaching skills takes *time*. Developing the many skills that promote positive effects on students is a lifelong endeavor. Once one gets comfortable in a situation, there is no growth, so teachers should beware of becoming comfortable. It is like motivation in which just enough frustration is introduced to make the learner want to get back into equilibrium. This "getting back into equilibrium" is where learning (growth) takes place.

After teaching skills related to student achievement have been identified, an effective process can be employed to learn these skills. A framework for acquiring teaching skills was offered by Joyce and Showers (1995). This framework includes theory exploration, demonstration, practice with accompanying feedback, and adaptation and generalization.

1. *Theory exploration.* As a professional, the teacher must first understand the research, theory, and reasoning behind the skills or strategies to be learned and the guiding principles that oversee their use. One way to do this is to further explore the skills through additional readings and discussions

with peers or colleagues. Reading and research will deflect the criticism that teaching does not have a knowledge base (see chapter 2).

2. *Demonstration.* In this phase, the new skill is modeled for the teacher. Examples of the skill in action may be conducted through a live demonstration by an expert, through videos, or computer simulations. "A familiar litany among student teachers is that their college professors never model the practices they verbally espouse. The absence of modeling must be anathema to effective supervisors and mentors in schools and universities" (Rieman & Thies-Sprinthall, 1998, p. 306).

3. *Practice with accompanying feedback.* It has often been said that the three most important things in real estate are location, location, and location. It can also be said that the three most important activities in developing teaching skills are practice, practice, and practice. A teacher, on the door to her instrumental music room, has mounted an attitude poster that reads,

> Pracktiss maakes perfeckt
> Praktiss maakes perfeckt
> Praktiss makes perfeckt
> Praktis makes perfeckt
> Practiss makes perfeckt
> Practiss makes perfect
> Practiss makes perfect
> Practice makes perfect

Whatever the situation, practice is required to develop any skill whether it is in the arts, sports, or teaching. The role of practicing cannot be overemphasized. The practice session should take place in a controlled environment and should be recorded through a video so that performance is documented.

Practice is most effective when it is performed with colleagues. As soon as possible after the practice session, feedback regarding performance should be received from colleagues. Immediate feedback allows teachers to become aware of parts of their performance that were successful and those that needed adjustment. Receiving this feedback prevents poor performance from becoming habitual.

Whenever the practicing situation warrants, microteaching should be employed. Microteaching is teaching a short lesson to a group of peers or colleagues concentrating on only a few skills, usually not more than three. The microteaching session should be video-recorded. Since a microteaching lesson is short and focuses on just a few skills, the teacher can specifically concentrate on developing just those particular skills and evaluating them readily. If the selected skills are those the teacher wants to acquire or increase, it is simple to count how many times they have appeared in the microteaching session. If the selected behaviors are those that should be eliminated, they also can be counted. Subsequent microteaching sessions can document the increase of desirable behaviors and the decrease of those that are undesirable. Practice under microteaching conditions can then continue until the desired level of achievement has been realized.

4. *Adaptation and generalization.* There is no point in developing skills positively correlated to student achievement if they are not actually implemented in the classroom. Once the skills have been practiced in a clinical setting, they can then be transferred to and practiced in an actual classroom environment. Video-recording remains a critical necessity. Afterwards, the teacher should receive feedback from peers, sooner rather than later. But it is still essential that the teacher self-evaluates.

ADDITIONAL WAYS TO DEVELOP PROFESSIONALLY

There are several general guidelines to help teachers and their colleagues develop professionally. The advice in these guidelines could be implemented as determined by colleagues.

- Try to develop personally. The more you develop *personally*, the more well-rounded you will be and the more enrichment you can bring to classrooms. Knowledge can be expanded by reading outside your field; traveling; pursuing hobbies; attending plays, concerts, ballets, and operas; and participating in sports.
- Remain current on general issues as well as those in your field and in education as a whole.
- Switch schools and/or grade or subject level periodically.
- Join a professional association/organization. An excellent source for identifying an organization that is appropriate for you and your group is the *Encyclopedia of Associations*. Organizations affiliated with education fall into two categories: general and specialty. Those in the general category cover issues and topics common to all teachers; those in the specialty category deal with a particular subject and/or grade level. In addition to publishing their own periodicals, general and specialty organizations commonly have conferences and exhibits teachers may attend. The conferences enable teachers to participate in workshops, locate relevant materials for their classrooms, and meet and interact with other teachers.

Most school districts budget for teachers to attend conferences and rotate which grades and/or subject areas will be represented each year. Teachers can then share the information gathered from the conference with other teachers in the district who have similar interests. Teachers could eventually plan to take leadership positions in organizations they may choose to join.[1]

- Network with other teachers to obtain new information to improve teaching or share common interests. These teachers may be in the same school, district, or found through the Internet.
- Visit other school districts and classes.

REFLECTIVE TEACHING

One of the most important professional development activities in which a teacher can be involved is reflective teaching. Reflective teaching is a comprehensive process that involves self-reflection, collaboration, and documentation.

1. *Self-reflection.* Self-reflection is also known as reflective thinking and self-evaluation. It is a critical tool for personal development. Self-reflection serves as a "stitch-in-time-saves-nine" for teachers, assisting them in becoming analytic/diagnostic so that poor procedures are not perpetuated and problems do not go unchecked before they get out of control. Personal and professional strengths are identified as well as skills needing development. Being a self-reflective teacher involves the attitudes of open-mindedness, intellectual and professional responsibility, and total immersion in the reflective process. It is a continuous process that must become an integral component of the daily life of a teacher. Self-reflection guides the four categories needed for professional development already presented in this chapter: individualization, teacher direction, context, and collaboration.

2. *Collaboration.* To be effective, reflective teaching should be implemented with the cooperation and participation of others. In addition to self-evaluation, cooperation and feedback should be sought from "buddies" (peers or colleagues) and *from learners themselves*. In the collaborative process, it is crucial that colleagues do not rubber-stamp each other but provide positive and corrective feedback. A lack of agreement among teachers, peers, and learners can often provide the personal dissonance needed to spur deeper investigation and growth.

Learners can offer useful information to teachers by deciding whether the lesson objective was achieved, if the method(s) and materials used by the teacher were helpful, how both could have been improved, and overall how the learners reacted to the lesson. Teachers should take some time to reflect and list other information learners can provide.

3. *Documentation.* For reflective teaching to be objective and concrete, the teaching needs to be *recorded*. This documentation is particularly important because it has been reported that there is a gap in perception between what teachers think they do in the classroom and what they actually do (Hook & Rosenshine, 1979). Also, it has been found that most teachers, even those selected by principals to be mentor teachers, those responsible for

developing new teachers, have a limited instructional repertoire, *relying on only one strategy*, thus preventing students from learning (Joyce & Showers, 1995). And principals themselves have been guilty of providing teachers with inflated and not particularly productive evaluations (Frase & Streshley, 1994). Documentation can be provided through reflective journals, portfolios, and guided observation instruments.

- *Reflective journals.* Reflective journals afford the teacher the opportunity to record on a daily basis a sequence of activities or events that occurs in the classroom. The teacher can then select one or more of these events to use for analytic and evaluative thinking. These events could include difficulty a student was having achieving the lesson objective, dealing with a new or chronic discipline problem, or analyzing routines that were causing confusion. The teacher could then write hard statements about what s/he learned and/or questions about what s/he needed to learn from that event, and how s/he could use that information in the future.
- *Portfolios.* Glatthorn (1996) defined portfolios as, "Systematic collections of materials selected and assembled by a professional and used to document professional accomplishments" (p. 31). A portfolio assists the teacher in determining effective performance within a specific context (Shulman, 1987). Portfolios are used primarily to chronicle teacher growth. The objective(s) of establishing the portfolio should be clear. It is not just a collection of the teacher's activities, but *a record of improvement or lack thereof.* Sources may come from the teachers themselves, from students (learners), colleagues, administrators, and parents. A common objective for preparing a portfolio is developing teaching skills. These skills are then documented by placing in the portfolio different relevant materials. These might include a video-recorded lesson that was not successful, then redone (and re-recorded) in a successful way as a result of what was learned from the first experience; pictures of students as they began developing a project or activity and then pictures of the final product itself; samples of student work that confirm achievement of objectives, especially pre-test and post-test samples that verify growth; unit plans; increasing teaching behaviors that are desirable and decreasing undesirable ones; and observations by peers. The portfolio also assists teachers in identifying strengths and weaknesses, and in this sense it is individualized for each teacher and helps the teacher capitalize on strengths as well as self-identify areas that need improvement.

As already indicated in chapter 7, coaching rubrics can be used to develop and document performance. These rubrics can be used for questioning skills, lesson and unit planning, classroom management, and a myriad of other teaching skills.

A coaching rubric can also be created for professional development, and as with all other rubrics, should be revised when necessary. The criteria for this rubric can be determined by all collaborators after they research what would reflect the best in professional development. As teachers progress in this development, they can complete the performance indicators. All coaching rubrics represent a universe of criteria. It is not necessary to implement all of them, but constant exposure to the criteria serves as a reminder of both outstanding performance and of criteria that could still be acted upon.

A collaborative team of teachers developed the criteria in the Coaching Rubric for Professional Development (Table 9.2). Note that it is coded (T), which means that it takes time to complete. For clarity of use, some of the performance indicators have been filled in. Blank performance indicators can offer criteria which will help teachers continue to grow.

When school districts and universities together take the time to think through teacher education and professional development programs to make them truly meaningful, teachers, students, and the nation will benefit. The ample resources currently available will be put to more productive use.

In addition, teaching will be on a professional par with medicine and law because the attributes that according to Saphier (1994) teaching currently lacks that would make it a full-fledged profession will have been addressed. These characteristics are as follows:

- Has a recognized knowledge base;
- Demands rigorous training and certification of its members;
- Fosters a culture of consultation and collaboration in the workplace;
- Systematically indoctrinates and "enculturates" new members;
- Requires that continuous, regular learning be built into the work cycle;
- Has high public accountability and takes full responsibility for outcomes; and
- Internally maintains high standards of practice.

Besides increasing the professionalization of teaching, a most significant result of teacher growth in their ability to deliver effective instruction is that student achievement will rise and student behavior problems will decline. These positive effects will reduce teacher stress and provide greater job satisfaction so that teachers can continue to perform the most important job in the world.

BLUEPRINT SUMMARY

- All TEC members are involved in creating professional development.

Effective Professional Development

Table 9.2. Coaching Rubric for Professional Development (T)

Criteria	Performance Indicators
the teacher identified reading for personal and professional broadening	identified *Classroom Instruction That Works* by Marzano, Pickering, and Pollack (2001)
read the materials and was able to describe what was learned	read text, learned that the nine major instructional strategies which affect student achievement are identifying similarities and differences, summarizing, reinforcing effort, homework and practice, using non-linguistic representations, cooperative learning, setting objectives, generating and testing hypotheses, and using questions, cues, and advance organizers
used the new learning acquired from the materials in the classroom	used similarities and differences when teaching verbs by comparing them with other verbs and contrasting them with other parts of speech
evaluated the effect of the new learning on instruction	evaluated students on subsequent test on which they performed significantly better than they had before I made the comparisons/contrasts and just gave them definitions and examples
identified a relevant professional association (or associations)	identified the Association for Supervision and Curriculum Development
joined the professional association(s)	joined Association for Supervision and Curriculum Development in June
participated in the association's activities and can describe what was learned	
transferred the new learning acquired from the professional association to the classroom and evaluated the effect of the new learning	
identified a mentor to assist in professional development	identified veteran master teacher Marian Floyd
identified others with whom to network	identified and contacted June Larson and Roy Pinzer from neighboring districts
identified ways to act as an agent to arrange for complementing teaching	
collaborated with colleagues to obtain feedback for self-reflection	collaborated with fellow fourth-grade teachers Lisa, Tom, and Frank

used guided observation for self-reflection	used the Coaching Rubric for Lesson Planning and Implementation with my colleagues to evaluate my video-recording
sought input from learners	sought input from class every Friday in both writing and in classroom discussion regarding how well the week went and what could be done to improve instruction on the part of both the students and myself
used a self-reflective journal	used a self-reflective journal to jot down what happened each day; arranged with Marian Floyd to discuss my journal once a week
developed a portfolio for self-reflection	
As a result of the above, identified own professional development needs	
devised a plan to meet the needs	
If learning a particular skill/model was identified as a need for development, explained the theory supporting the skill/model	
If necessary, arranged to have the skill/model demonstrated by an expert or video simulation	
practiced the skill/model with feedback (under microteaching conditions where applicable) until a desired level of achievement was attained	
implemented that skill/model in the classroom	
evaluated the implementation of that skill/model in the classroom	
identified new areas for professional development	

- A professional development coordinator is appointed to oversee the process, avoid the universal pitfalls of unsuccessful attempts at professional development, and evaluate the program annually. The coordinator is accountable for the program.

- Universities develop new specialty programs that provide a comprehensive solid curriculum for the role of professional development coordinator.

- The professional development process has *all* of the following characteristics: individualization, teacher direction, context, and collaboration.

- Skills to be developed for teachers and administrators include theory exploration, demonstration, practice with accompanying feedback, and adaptation and generalization.

- All teachers are involved in reflective teaching. This process is characterized by self-reflection, collaboration, and documentation. Documentation is collected through reflective journals and portfolios.

NOTE (FOR PAGE 123)

1. Simply belonging to an organization does not make a teacher a professional. Teachers must be willing to learn new concepts and processes that are effective, share them with colleagues, and *implement and evaluate the new learning in their classrooms.*

References

Abutaleb, Y. (2012, July 27). School dress codes aren't just for students anymore. *USAToday*. http://usatoday30.usatoday.com/money/media/story/2012-07-17/teacher-dress-code/56579488/1.

Adams, C. (2014, February 10). K-12 and higher education often fail to collaborate effectively, survey says. Education Week's Blogs, College Bound.

Aguilar, E. (2013, September 8). Tips for coaching new teachers. *Education Week Teacher*. Teacher Blogs, The Art of Coaching Teachers.

Aguilar, E. (2015, June 22). 5 characteristics of an effective school team. *Edutopia*.

American Association of Colleges for Teacher Education. (1976). *Educating a profession: Profile of a beginning teacher*. Washington, DC: Author.

American Educational Research Association. (2005, June 20). *Studying teacher education: The report of the AERA panel on research on teacher education*. Author.

American Educational Research Association. (2013a, May 28). 10 costly mistakes commonly made by teaching candidates. Education Week's Blogs, Career Corner.

American Educational Research Association. (2013b, June 10). Interview questions-Part II, professional educator. Education Week's Blogs, Career Corner.

Anderson, S. (2013, October 9). Achieving expert instruction on a large scale. Education Week's Blogs, International Perspectives on Education Reform.

Auguste, B., Kihn, P., & Miller, M. (2010, September). Closing the talent gap: Attracting and retaining top-third graduates to careers in teaching, pp. 1-8, Social Sector Office, McKinsey & Co.

Bangert-Drowns, R., Kulik, R., & Kulik, C. (1991). Effects of frequent classroom testing. *Journal of Educational Research*, 85, 88–99.

Barker, J., Semenov, A., Michaelson, L., Provan, L., Snyder, H., & Munakata, Y. (2014, June 17). Less-structured time in children's daily lives predicts self-directed executive functioning. *Frontiers*. http://journal.frontiersin.org/Journal/10.3389/fpsyg.2014.00593/full.

Baron M., & Boschee, F. (1996, April). Dispelling the myths surrounding OBE. *Phi Delta Kappan*, 574–76.

Barth, R. (1990). *Improving our schools from within*. San Francisco: Jossey Bass.

Basu, K. (2012, March 29). Ending the first Ed.D. program. *Inside Higher Education*.

Blumenstyk, G. (2015a, June 16). After years lambasting teacher-ed programs, Art Levine creates one. *The Chronicle of Higher Education*. http://chronicle.com/article/After-Years-Lambasting/230931/.

Blumenstyk, G. (2015b, June 16). Video: Teacher-education critic turns graduate-school creator. *The Chronicle of Higher Education*. http://chronicle.com/article/Video-A-Teacher-Education/230929/?cid=at&utm_source=at&utm_medium=en.

Brody, L. (2015, August 4). Study questions value of teacher development. *The Wall Street Journal.* http://www.wsj.com/articles/study-questions-value-of-teacher-development-1438696823.

Brookhart, S. (2004). *Grading.* Upper Saddle River, NJ: Pearson Education.

Chall, J. (2000). *The academic achievement challenge: What really works in the classroom.* New York: Guilford.

Chesley, G., & Jordan, J. (2012, May). What's missing from teacher prep. *Educational Leadership*, 69(8), 41–45.

Chetty, R., Friedman, J., & Rockoff, J. (2012, January). *The long-term impacts of teachers: Teacher value-added and student outcomes in adulthood*, NBER Working Paper No. 17699, JEL No. I2, J24.

Danielson, C. (1996). *Enhancing professional practice: A framework for teaching.* Alexandria, VA: Association for Supervision and Curriculum Development.

Darling-Hammond, L. (1995, Fall). Changing conceptions of teacher development. *Teacher Education Quarterly*, 9–26.

DeWitt, P. (2014, August 28). Are you prepared to be a cooperating teacher? Education Week's Blogs, Finding Common Ground.

Diaz-Maggioli, G. (2004). *Teacher-centered professional development.* Alexandria, VA: Association for Supervision and Curriculum Development.

Duncan, A. (2011, August). Forge a commitment to authentic professional learning. *The Learning Forward Journal*, 32(4), 70–72.

Ellis, D. (2000). Becoming a master student, 9th ed. Boston: Houghton Mifflin.

Ellis, A. (2001). *Research on educational innovations*, 3rd ed. Larchmont, New York: Eye on Education.

Felch, J., Song, J., & Poindexter, S. (2010, December 22). In reforming schools, quality of teaching often overlooked, *Los Angeles Times*, 4.

Ferlazzo, L. (2014, September 14). Response: Teachers should dress as student's advocate, not peer. *Education Week Teacher.* Teacher Blogs, Classroom Q&A with Larry Ferlazzo.

Ferlazzo, L. (2015, March 17). Response: "Every teacher is a language teacher." *Education Week Teacher.* Teacher Blogs, Classroom Q&A with Larry Ferlazzo.

Ferrett, S. (1997). *Peak performance: Success in college and beyond.* New York: McGraw-Hill.

Fitzhugh, W. (2006, October 20). Master of none. *The Concord Review.*

Frase, L., & Streshley, W. (1994). Lack of accuracy, feedback, and commitment in teacher evaluation. *Journal of Personnel Evaluation in Education*, 1, 47–57.

Fuhrman, T. (2015, July 14). Training faculty for mobile learning. *1105 Media Inc.*, Ed-Tech Group.

Fryshman, B. (2014, August 11). Let's be honest: We don't know how to make great teachers. Education Week online. http://www.edweek.org/tm/articles/2014/08/11/fp_fryshman_teacher_quality/html. Fuller, F. (1969). Concerns of teachers: A developmental conceptualization. *American Educational Research Journal*, 6(2), 206–66.

Gardner, W. (2014a, August 18). Best teaching is based on relationships. Education Week's Blogs, Walt Gardner's Reality Check.

Gardner, W. (2014b, September 10). What makes a teacher great? Education Week's Blogs, Walt Gardner's reality check.

Gardner, W. (2015, April 20). Personality tests for teacher candidates. Education Week's Blogs, Walt Gardner's Reality Check.

Glatthorn, A. (1996). *The teacher's portfolio: Fostering and documenting professional development.* Rockport, MA: Pro>Active Publications.

Glickman, C. (1992, September). The essence of school renewal: The prose has begun. *Educational Leadership*, 24–27.

Goodwin, L. (2015, February 3). Duncan's teacher ed proposals miss the mark. Education Week blogs, OpEducation.

Goral, T. (2015, July 20). Why K-12 education needs diverse teachers. *District Administration.* http://www.districtadministration.com/article/why-k12-education-needs-diverse-teachers.

Green, E. (2010, March 7). Building a better teacher. *The New York Times Magazine*, MM30.

Hall, G. E., Wallace, R., & Dossett, W. A. (1973). *A developmental conceptualization of the adoption process within educational institutions*. Austin: Research and Development Center for Teacher Education, University of Texas.

Hall, G. E., & Loucks, S. (1978, September). Teacher concerns as a basis for facilitating and personalizing staff development. *Teachers College Record*, 80, 36–53.

Hanushek, E. (2011, April 6). Recognizing the value of good teachers. *Education Week*, 30(27), 34–35.

Harris, E. (2015, June 5). Judge rules second version of New York teachers' exam is also racially biased. *The New York Times*, A15.

Haycock, K. (1998). Good teaching matters . . . a lot. *Thinking K-16*, 3(2), 1–14.

Heiten, L. (2013, August 1). Poll: Teacher engagement starts low, worsens with time. Education Week's Teacher Blogs, Teaching Now.

Henchey, S. (2011, July 25). What I learned from my first student teacher. *Education Week* Teacher online.

Hook, C., & Rosenshine, B. (1979). Accuracy of teacher reports of their classroom behavior. *Review of Educational Research*, 49, 1–12.

Jackson, R. (2015, May 26). *Five of the biggest mistakes I made as a new teacher*. ASCD Edge.

Jensen, E. (1998). *Teaching with the brain in mind*. Alexandria, VA: Association for Supervision and Curriculum Development.

Jensen, E. (2005). *Teaching with the brain in mind*, 2nd ed. Alexandria, VA: Association for Supervision and Curriculum Development.

Joyce, B., & Showers, B. (1995). *Student achievement through staff development*, 2nd ed. New York: Longman.

Joyce, B., & Showers, B. (2002). *Student achievement through staff development*, 3rd ed. Alexandria, VA: Association for Supervision and Curriculum Development.

Kika, F., McLaughlin, T., & Dixon, J. (1992). Effects of frequent testing of secondary algebra students. *Journal of Educational Research*, 85, 159–62.

Kimpston, R. D. (1987). Teacher and principal state of concern regarding implementation of benchmark testing: A longitudinal study. *Teaching and Teacher Education*, 3(3), 205–17.

Kozloff, M. (2002). Ed schools in crisis. Watson School of Education. University of North Carolina at Wilmington, http://people.uncut.edu/kozloffm/.

Kramer, R. (2008). *Ed follies: The miseducation of America's teachers*. New York: Author's Guild.

Labaree, D. (2008). An uneasy relationship: A history of teacher education in the university. In Cochran-Smith, M., Feiman-Nemser, S., & McIntyre, J. (Eds.). *Handbook of Research on Teacher Education: Enduring Issues in Education*, 290–306.

Lankford, H., Loeb, S., McEachin, A., Miller, L., & Wycoff, J. (2014, December). Who enters teaching? Encouraging evidence that the status of teaching is improving. *Educational Researcher*, American Educational Research Association, 43(9), 444–53.

Lazear, D. (1998). *The rubrics way: Using MI to assess understanding*. Tuscon, AZ: Zephyr Press.

Leibman, P. (2015). *Launch a teaching career: Secrets for aspiring teachers*. Lanham, MD: Rowman and Littlefield.

Lemov, D. (2015). *Teach like a champion 2.0: 62 techniques that put students on the path to college*. San Francisco: Jossey-Bass.

Leo, J. (2005, October 24). Class(room) warriors. *US News and World Report*.

Levine, A. (2011, May 8), The new normal of teacher education. *The Chronicle of Higher Education*. http://chronicle.com/article/The-New-Normal-of-Teacher/127430/.

Link, L. (2012, January 31). Teaching ahead: A roundtable. Education Week's Blogs. edweek.org/teachers/teaching_ahead/how-would-you-change-teacher-prep/.

Marks, M. (2000, January 9). Education Life. *The New York Times*, 16–17.

Marzano, R. (2003). *What works in schools: Translating research into action*. Alexandria, VA: Association for Supervision and Curriculum Development.

Marzano, R. (2007). *The art and science of teaching: A comprehensive framework for effective instruction*. Alexandria, VA: Association for Supervision and Curriculum Development.

Marzano, R. (2009, September). Setting the record straight on "high-yield" strategies. *Phi Delta Kappan*, 91(1), 33–37.

Marzano, R., Pickering, D., & Pollack, J. (2001). *Classroom instruction that works: Research-based strategies for increasing student achievement*. Alexandria, VA: Association for Supervision and Curriculum Development.

Matthews, J. (2010, October 1). Ed school professors resist teaching practical skills. The Answer Sheet, WashingtonPost.com.

Mission, E. (2014, February 26). A strong start for teachers. Education Week's Blogs, Global Learning.

Mizell, H. (2013, July 16). Superintendents need a new view on professional learning. *Education Week*, Teacher Blogs, Learning Forward's PD Watch.

Molnar, M. (2015, March 18). "Education innovation clusters" aim to improve schools. *Education Week*, 34(24), 12.

Moore, R. (2011). Brown vs. the African American teacher. *The American Public School Teacher: Past, Present, and Future*. Drury, D. & Baker, J. (Eds.), Harvard Education Press.

Morris, M. (2015, May 19). Liberals Dominate Commencement Speakers' Circuit in 2015, Outnumber Conservatives 6-1. http://cnsnews.com/.

Morrison, N. (2015, June 10). The eight components of great professional development. *Forbes*. http://www.forbes.com/sites/nickmorrison/2015/06/10/the-eight-components-of-great-professional-development/2/.

National Association of Secondary School Principals. (1996). *Breaking ranks: Changing an American institution*. Reston, VA: Author.

National Commission on Teaching and America's Future. (1996). *What matters most: Teaching for America's future*. New York: Carnegie Foundation.

National Commission on Teaching and America's Future. (2007). The high cost of teacher turnover, Policy brief. ERIC Number: ED498001, author.

National Network of State Teachers of the Year (2013, April 17). Professionalizing teaching: Five paradigms missing from teaching. Author.

Nettles, M., Scatton, L., Steinberg, J., & Tyler, L. (2011). *Performance and passing rate differences of African American and white prospective teachers on PraxisTM examinations: A joint project of the National Education Association (NEA) and Educational Testing Service (ETS)*. Princeton, NJ: Educational Testing Service.

Nosich, G. (2009). *Learning to think things through: A guide to critical thinking across the curriculum*, 3rd ed. Upper Saddle River, NJ: Prentice-Hall.

Nye, B., Konstantopoulos, S., & Hedges, L. (2004, Fall). How large are teacher effects? *Educational Evaluation and Policy Analysis*, 26(3), 237–57.

O'Brien, J. (2013, May 19). School adminstrators' advice for teaching candidates. American Association for Employment in Education. Education Week's Blogs, Career Corner.

Pagliaro, M. (2012). *Research-based unit and lesson planning: Maximizing student achievement*. Lanham, MD: Rowman and Littlefield.

Paul, R., & Elder, L. (2001). *Critical thinking: Tools for taking charge of your learning and your life*. Upper Saddle River, NJ: Prentice Hall.

Paul, R., & Elder, L. (2008). *The miniature guide to critical thinking concepts and tools*. Dillon Beach, CA: Foundation for Critical Thinking.

Phelps P. H. (1993). Bringing in the new: An induction ceremony for new teachers. *The Clearing House*, 66(3), 154.

Pipho, C. (1998, January). The value-added side of standards. *Phi Delta Kappan*, 341–42.

Pondiscio, R. & Stringer, K. (2015, October 7). Reforming ed schools from within. *Common Core Watch*, The Thomas B. Fordham Institute.

Popham, J. (2000). *Testing! Testing!* Boston: Allyn and Bacon.

Quartz (2014). http://qz.com/334926/your-college-major-is-a-pretty-good-indication-of-how-smart-you-are/.

Ravitch, D. (1985, September 4). Major trends in research: 22 scholars report on their fields. *Chronicle of Higher Education*, 2–9.

Ravitch, D. (2003, August 23). A brief history of teacher professionalism. White House Conference on Preparing Tomorrow's Teachers.

Resmovits, J. (2013, October 30). Starting teacher SAT scores rise as educators face tougher evaluations. *Huffington Post*.
Rieman, A., & Thies-Sprinthall, L. (1998). *Mentoring and supervision for teacher development*. New York: Longman.
Rinke, W. (1997, September). How to be a winner. *Family Circle*, 10.
Robbins, P. (2015). *Peer coaching to enrich professional practice, school culture, and student learning*. Alexandria, VA: Association for Supervision and Curriculum Development.
Robinson, S. (2015, March). Cause for concern at teaching colleges. *District Administration*.
Ronfeldt, M., Loeb, S., & Wyckoff, J. (2012, January). How teacher turnover harms student achievement. National Center for Analysis of Longitudinal Data in Education Research, Working Paper 70.
Rothman, R. (1997, December). KERA: A tale of one school. *Phi Delta Kappan*, 272–75.
Runté, R. (1995). *Thinking About Teaching: An Introduction.* Taylor, G., & Runté, R. Eds. Toronto: Harcourt Brace.
Russert, T. (2001, May 20th). Commencement address delivered at Dominican College, Orangeburg, NY.
Ryan, K., Cooper, J., & Tauer, S. (2008). *Teaching for student learning: Becoming a master teacher*. Boston: Houghton Mifflin.
Sackstein, S. (2015a, March 6). Everyday essential apps for education. *Education Week Teacher*, Teacher Blogs, Work in Progress.
Sackstein, S. (2015b, May 28). The perfect teaching candidate. *Education Week Teacher*, Teacher Blogs, Work in Progress.
Sanchez, C. (2015, May 8). What the best college teachers do. How Learning Happens, nprED.
Sanchez, C., & Summers, J. (2014, June 17). Study delivers failing grades for many programs training teachers. How Learning Happens, nprEd.
Sanders, W., & Rivers, J. (1996). *Cumulative and residual effects of teachers on future student academic achievement*. Research progress report. Knoxville: University of Tennessee Value-Added Research and Assessment Center.
Saphier, J. (1994). Bonfires and magic bullets: Making teaching a true profession. Research for Better Teaching, Inc.
Sawchuk, S. (2010, September 29). "Churn, ambivalence, confusion" in teacher ed? Education Week's Blogs, Teacher Beat.
Sawchuk, S. (2012, March 23). Report probes the "diversity gap" on teacher tests. Education Weeks Blogs, Teacher Beat.
Sawchuk, S. (2013, April 12). AACTE critiques proposed accreditation standards. Education Week's Blogs, Teacher Beat.
Sawchuk, S. (2015a, March 5). Teacher education group asserts "crisis of confidence" in accreditor. Education Week's Blogs, Teacher Beat.
Sawchuk, S. (2015b, April 28). Gates foundation to expand teacher-preparation grantmaking. Education Week's Blogs, Teacher Beat.
Sawchuk, S. (2015c, May 7). In surprise move, teacher ed. accreditation group ousts president. Education Week's Blogs, Teacher Beat.
Schaffhauser, D. (2015, February 26). Report: New teacher prep rules "too stringent." *The Journal*, http://thejournal.com/articles/2015/02/26/new-teacher-prep-rules-too-stringent.aspx.
Schmidt, W. (2014, October 28). Improving quality teacher prep programs in mathematics. *The Intersection*, The Hunt Institute Blogs.
Schmoker, M. (2011). *Focus: Elevating the essentials to radically improve student learning*. Alexandria, VA: Association for Supervision and Curriculum Development.
Schmoker, M. (2013, June 4). The lost art of teaching soundly structured lessons. Education Week Teacher online.
Schneider, J. (2015, April 15). A national strategy to improve the teaching profession. *Education Week*, 34(27), 20-21.
Schramm, Michael. (2015, June 8). Jerry Seinfeld says comedians avoid college gigs, students are "so PC." *USA Today*.

Shulman, L. S. (1987). Knowledge and teaching: Foundations of the new reform. *Harvard Educational Review*, 19(2), 4–14.

Sims, W. (2014). Teacher quality is a new national-security issue. *Education Week*, 33(27), 29, 31.

Sparks, S. (2012, April 25). Studies test for ways to spot good teachers. *Education Week*, 31(29), 12.

Stansbury, M. (2015, July 14). How a dashboard can improve the quality of teachers. *eCampus News*. http://www.ecamusnews.com.

Stern, (2006, Summer). The ed schools' latest—and worst—humbug: Teaching for "social justice" is a cruel hoax on disadvantaged kids. *City Journal*.

Stiggens, R. (2005a). Assessment crisis: The absence of assessment FOR learning. *Phi Delta Kappan*, 83(10), 758–65.

Stiggens, R. (2005b). *Student-involved assessment FOR learning*, 4th ed. Upper Saddle River, NJ: Pearson/Merrill Prentice Hall.

Stotsky, S. (2006, Summer). Ed schools: The shame of the nation. *Academic Questions*, 18(3), 44–53.

Stratford, M. (2015, January 5). Higher education groups criticize education department estimate of how much teacher prep regulations will cost. *Inside Higher Education*. https://insidehighered.com.

Stronge, J. (2007). *Qualities of effective teachers*, 2nd ed. Alexandria, VA: Association for Supervision and Curriculum Development.

Superville, D. (2015, May 1). Video series highlights how successful principals do their jobs. Education Weeks's Blogs, District Dossier.

Sylvestre, S. (2015, May 5). Six do's and don't's for student teachers. American Association for Employment in Education. Education Week's Blogs, Career Corner.

Thomas, L. (2013, September 4). 10 good ways to ensure bad professional learning. Learning Forward, Teacher Blogs, Learning Forward's PD Watch.

Tierney, J. (2013, January 17). Anybody? anybody? What Ferris Bueller got right. *The Atlantic*.

Troen, V., & Boles, K. (2003). *Who's teaching your children?* New Haven: Yale University Press.

U.S. Department of Education (2014, November 25). New rules build on reforms and innovation efforts to ensure educators are classroom-ready. Press Office, press@ed.gov.

Walsh, K. (2006, March 16). Coming up empty. *National Council on Teacher Quality*, 3(1), 1–5.

Ward, W. A. (n.d.). To risk. http://www.appleseeds.org/to-risk_WAW.htm

Welch, J. (2000). *GE strategy and performance . . . as reported to share owners 1980 to 2000*. Fairfield, CT: GE Corporation.

Wiggins, G. (1998). *Educative assessment: Designing assessments to inform and improve student performance*. San Francisco: Jossey-Bass.

Will, G. (2013, April 4). Propaganda as pedagogy. *The Palm Beach Post*, reprinted from *The Washington Post*.

Williams, W. (2013, March 13). Education rot. TownHall.com.

Wong, H., & Wong, R. (1998). *The first days of school*. Mountain View, CA: Harry K. Wong Publications.

Woolfolk, A. (2008). *Educational psychology*, 10th ed. Boston: Pearson.

Wright, A. (2014, November 19). Teachers need more feedback from other teachers. *Education Week*, Teacher Blogs, Teaching Ahead: A Roundtable.

Wright, S., Horn, S., & Sanders, W. (1997). Teacher and classroom context effects on student achievement: Implications for teacher evaluation. *Journal of Personnel Evaluation in Education*, 11, 57–67.

Zalaznick, M. (2015, July 20). School neuroscience unleashes students' brain power. *District Administration*. http://www.districtadministration.com/article/neuroscience-builds-students-brain-power.

www.ingramcontent.com/pod-product-compliance
Lightning Source LLC
Chambersburg PA
CBHW030115010526
44116CB00005B/263